A FEAST OF CREATURES

A Feast of Creatures

ANGLO-SAXON RIDDLE-SONGS

Translated
with Introduction,
Notes and Commentary
by
Craig Williamson

The University of Pennsylvania Press
Philadelphia   1982

Library of Congress Cataloging in Publication Data

Exeter book. Selections. English. 1982.
  A feast of creatures.

  Chiefly translations from: The Old English
riddles of the Exeter book/edited by Craig
Williamson. ©1977.
  Bibliography: p.
  Includes index
  1. Riddles, Anglo-Saxon—Translations into
English. 2. Songs, Anglo-Saxon—Texts—Transla-
tions into English. 3. Anglo-Saxon poetry—
Translations into English. 4. English poetry—
Translations from Anglo-Saxon. I. Williamson,
Craig, 1943–   . II. Exeter book.
Selections. 1977. Old English riddles of the
Exeter book.
PR1762.W5 1982   829'.1   82–4907
ISBN 0–8122–7843–7   AACR2

Printed in the United States of America

The translations are dedicated to:
The dark-eyed lady of the jade wood,
The gold warbler, the stripling queen,
The dancing red fox full of head-rhymes,
The mind-spider spinning dreams,
And the spirit that delights in the Other.

CONTENTS

ACKNOWLEDGMENTS

Research on portions of the book was funded by the American Council of Learned Societies, the Andrew W. Mellon Foundation, and Swarthmore College. Thanks go to my friends at Swarthmore and elsewhere who read portions of the book and offered suggestions—Charles Balestri, Mark Booth, John Hinchey, Marie Nelson, Joseph Patwell, James Rosier, Bernard Smith, Paula Smith, Susan Snyder, Philip Weinstein, and Susan Williamson.

CREDITS

Company, Inc., New York, N.Y.; Gary Snyder, *Earth House Hold* (New Directions, 1969), © 1969 by Gary Snyder, reprinted by permission of New Directions Publishing Corporation; Christopher Tolkien, ed. and tr., *The Saga of King Heidrek the Wise* (Thomas Nelson, 1960); William Carlos Williams, *Paterson* (New Directions, 1963), © 1949 by William Carlos Williams, reprinted by permission of New Directions Publishing Corporation; Craig Williamson, "Two Riddles," *College English* 35 (1974), and ed., *The Old English Riddles of the Exeter Book* (University of North Carolina Press, 1977); William Butler Yeats, selections from "The Wild Swans at Coole," reprinted by permission of Macmillan Publishing Co., Inc. from *Collected Poems* of William Butler Yeats, © 1919 by Macmillan Publishing Co., Inc., renewed 1947 by Bertha Georgie Yeats, and by permission of A. P. Watt Ltd.

ILLUSTRATIONS

The illustrations used in this book are taken from George Speake, *Anglo-Saxon Animal Art and Its Germanic Background*, © 1980 by Oxford University Press and are reprinted with the permission of the publisher. The plate numbers and original sources for the Speake drawings are as follows: Cover illustrations (from top to bottom): (1) portion of figure 10.e, gilt-bronze harness mount, Hardingstone, Northants; (2) figure 6.m, triangular buckle, Faversham, Kent; (3) figure 6.o, ornament detail from bronze work-box, Burwell, Gr. 42, Cambs.; (4) figure 6.r, gilt-bronze mount, Asthall, Oxon. The title page illustration is figure 14.b, panel of ornament, *Book of Durrow*, fo. 192, Trinity College, Dublin; the section title page illustrations are each figure 15.a, drinking-cup mouthpiece, Sutton Hoo ship-burial, Suffolk.

 **Part One**

INTRODUCTION

> Across time the ox's skin and the dart
> Of once-wing from horn to page preserve
> The song-smith's hammer, fire, din—
> Who were the Anglo-Saxon riddlers
> Who locked in the dark mirror of metaphor
> A cultural eye, an ageless game?
> Children do this and dying men—
> Creation sings in the cow's dead skin:
> Bound in another, all things begin.

The Old English riddles are a metaphoric and metamorphic celebration of life in the eye of the Anglo-Saxon. Metaphoric because each riddlic creature takes on the guise of another: the nightingale is an evening poet, mead is a wrestler, the sword a celibate thane, the silver wine-cup a seductress. Metamorphic because in the natural flow all creatures shift shapes: the horn turns from twinned head-warrior of the wild aurochs to battle-singer or mead-belly—sometimes it swallows the blood of hawthorn and gives to quill and vellum page the gift of words. The book too has its own beginnings —it sings in riddle 24:

A life-thief stole my world-strength,
Ripped off flesh and left me skin,
Dipped me in water and drew me out,
Stretched me bare in the tight sun;
The hard blade, clean steel, cut,
Scraped—fingers folded, shaped me.
Now the bird's once wind-stiff joy
Darts often to the horn's dark rim,
Sucks wood-stain, steps back again—
With a quick scratch of power, tracks
Black on my body, points trails.

The metaphor of riddles mirrors metamorphosis: all things shift in the body of nature and the mind of man. But the flow, the form and movement, remains. As the mind shifts, it shapes meaning. When is an iceberg a witch-warrior? When it curses and slaughters ships. When is it a great mother? When transformed and lifted, it rains down. There is a primitive participation and poetic synchronicity in this. Man charts the world and the world sings in images his uncharted spirit. The riddles are primitive flower and lyric seed. To us they offer a world in which there is an eye (I) in every other, a charged world where as Walt Whitman says, there is "God in every object."[2] If we no longer see the tree in the table or sense the sinuous vine in the wine's work or quicken in the bow of the nightingale's song, this may be a world we need.

ORIGINS

The riddles rest in a thousand-year-old vellum manuscript known as the Exeter Book which resides in Exeter Cathedral Library (skin songs in a holy

1. All translations of Old English poetry are my own. The original texts for riddles may be found in my text edition, *The Old English Riddles of the Exeter Book* (Chapel Hill: University of North Carolina Press, 1977); for nonriddlic poems, in *The Anglo-Saxon Poetic Records* (hereafter *ASPR*), ed. George Philip Krapp and Elliott Van Kirk Dobbie, 6 vols. (New York: Columbia University Press, 1931–53). Occasionally I have consulted other editions in making my translations from *ASPR*.

2. Walt Whitman, "Song of Myself," stanza 148, *Leaves of Grass*, ed. Harold W. Blodgett and Sculley Bradley (New York: W. W. Norton and Co., 1973), p. 86.

house). The scribal hand of the book dates from the late tenth century. Leofric, first Bishop of Exeter, donated the "great English book with variously wrought songs"[3] to the cathedral library in the eleventh century. The riddles were probably first written down in the late seventh or eighth centuries—or even in the ninth. How far back into oral tradition some of them go remains an open question. Who first chanted or wrote the riddles we may never know. Cynewulf, whose runic signature appears in two of the Exeter Book poems, was once thought to be author of the riddles; on stylistic grounds this now seems unlikely. Aldhelm of Malmesbury, the seventh-century English churchman who wrote one hundred Latin riddles, may have written some of the Old English riddle-songs. His love of vernacular poetry was legendary. He is said by William of Malmesbury to have charmed Anglo-Saxons into church by chanting Old English songs from a wayside bridge.[4] Aldhelm sent his Latin riddles and a treatise on verse to King Aldfrith of Northumbria, and the good king (who during his Irish exile turned out verse as the bard Flann Fina) may have responded in kind. The ninth-century soldier-scholar King Alfred, who admired Aldhelm's verse, may have honored his literary forebear with a riddle or two. But these are only guesses—the parentage of riddles is lost in time. Like most of their siblings in the Exeter Book, they remain anonymous voices of an age. As the book or singer of riddle 91 says: "Though the children of earth eagerly seek / To trace my trail, sometimes my tracks are dim."[5]

The manuscript itself is of little help in tracing the origin of riddles. The Exeter Book looks like an eclectic anthologist's choice of Old English verse. The ninety-odd riddles (the exact number depends on editorial grouping of related segments) occur in two main sections. The book also contains religious poetry ranging from the long tripartite treatment of Christ to the Old English "Phoenix" and "Physiologus" (including panther, whale, and partridge); saints' lives such as "Guthlac" and "Juliana"; poems in the elegiac mode (laments with or without Christian consolation) such as "The

3. A description (translated from the Old English) of the Exeter Book which appears in a list of Leofric's donations to the cathedral at the beginning of the book.

4. William of Malmesbury, *Gesta Pontificum Anglorum*, ed. N. E. S. A. Hamilton (London: Longman, 1870 [Rolls Series 52]), p. 336.

5. For more on the problems of authorship and date of the Exeter Book riddles, see the introduction to my text edition noted above.

Wanderer," "The Seafarer," and "The Wife's Lament"; the heroic "Wid-sith" and "Deor"; gnomic and homiletic verse such as "Precepts" and the "Exeter Maxims"; and the lyrically enigmatic "Wulf and Eadwacer," once thought to be a clue to the Cynewulfian authorship of riddles, now held to be a dramatic soliloquy like "The Wife's Lament." The Exeter Book itself is a rare creature—one of four surviving major manuscripts of Old English poetry.[6] In a medieval world where Latin manuscripts were primarily cherished by the religious scribes who copied them and monastic libraries which held them, and where all manuscripts were considered food for the fire by marauding Norsemen—the survival of the Exeter Book is something of a miracle. The book is scorched and stained and suffers from hard use; some of its pages are missing. Like some bizarrely shape-shifting riddle-creature, it seems to have been used variously as a cutting-board, a hot-plate, a beer-mat, and a filing cabinet for gold leaf. After this inglorious service, it lay song-dormant in library sleep until the nineteenth century when its contents were transcribed, edited, translated, and anthologized.

The poems of the Exeter Book were first edited by Benjamin Thorpe in 1842.[7] The first systematic attempt to solve all of the riddles came with Franz Dietrich's articles in 1859 and 1865.[8] The riddles were first edited as a separate text with full critical apparatus by Frederick Tupper in 1910.[9] Later editions of the Exeter Book by Christian W. M. Grein, Bruno Assmann, W. S. Mackie, and George Philip Krapp and Elliot Van Kirk Dobbie, and riddle editions by A. J. Wyatt and Moritz Trautmann helped to establish a text and to provide a proper critical context in which to read the riddles.[10] Riddle translators have included poets and scholars (many of

6. The other manuscripts are the Vercelli Book, the Junius Manuscript, and the Beowulf Codex.

7. Benjamin Thorpe, ed., *Codex Exoniensis: A Collection of Anglo-Saxon Poetry* (Society of Antiquaries of London, 1842).

8. F. Dietrich, "Die Räthsel des Exeterbuchs," *Zeitschrift für deutsches Altertum* 11 (1859): 448–90; 12 (1865): 232–52.

9. Frederick Tupper, Jr., ed., *The Riddles of the Exeter Book* (Boston: Ginn and Co., 1910).

10. Christian W. M. Grein, ed., *Bibliothek der angelsächsischen Poesie*, vol. 2 (Göttingen: G. H. Vigand, 1858); Bruno Assmann, ed., *Bibliothek der angelsächsischen Poesie*, vol. 3 (Göttingen: G. H. Vigand, 1898); W. S. Mackie, ed. and tr., *The Exeter Book*, pt. 2 (London: Early English Text Society, 1934); George Philip Krapp and Elliott Van Kirk Dobbie, eds., *The Exeter Book* (New York: Columbia University Press, 1936); A. J. Wyatt, ed., *Old English Riddles* (Boston: D. C. Heath, 1912); Moritz Trautmann, ed., *Die altenglischen Rätsel: Die*

whom are quoted in the final section of this introduction); translators of the full corpus include Mackie, Paull F. Baum, and Kevin Crossley-Holland.[11] My own edition of the riddles appeared in 1977;[12] my translations here are the first to be based on this most recent text. Occasionally, poets like Richard Wilbur have not only translated riddles but written their own (the importance of riddling to a modern poetic tradition is discussed briefly below in the section, "Poetry and the Primitive"). Thus does the Exeter Book offer not only an eye onto the medieval world but an ancient means of perceiving our own.

SOURCES AND ANALOGUES

The Old English riddles are the first and finest vernacular riddles of the Middle Ages. Although little is known about the possible social contexts of oral riddling in early Anglo-Saxon England, the riddles are presumably a wedding of oral practice and Latin literary tradition. Both a religious doctrine and a literary tradition were brought to England by Christian missionaries who carried with the gift of script, the Word of God. But as was true of many other Christian traditions, the literary riddle was transformed by the Anglo-Saxons into something uniquely their own.

The father of medieval Latin riddle poetry is Symphosius, an author of the fourth or fifth century whose identity remains obscure. He composed a century of riddles (set of one hundred), each three lines long, each bearing an entitled solution. His riddles influenced the Anglo-Latin riddle writers —mainly Aldhelm (640–709), Abbot of Malmesbury and later Bishop of Sherborne, who wrote his own century of Latin riddles (and may have written some of the Old English); Tatwine (d. 734), Archbishop of Canterbury, who wrote forty Latin riddles; and Eusebius (d. 747), now thought

---

Rätsel des Exeterbuchs (Heidelberg: C. Winter, 1915). For a fuller discussion of the various critical editions, see my text edition of 1977 noted above.

11. Mackie, *The Exeter Book*, pt. 2; Paull F. Baum, tr., *Anglo-Saxon Riddles of the Exeter Book* (Durham, N. C.: Duke University Press, 1963); Kevin Crossley-Holland, tr., *The Exeter Riddle Book* (London: Folio Society, 1978), reissued as *The Exeter Book Riddles* (New York: Penguin, 1979).

12. Williamson, *The Old English Riddles of the Exeter Book*.

to be Hwaetberht, Abbot of Wearmouth and a friend of Bede, who wrote sixty. Other Anglo-Latin riddle writers include Alcuin, Boniface, and a handful of anonymous poets (possibly including Bede himself). The influence of Latin riddles on the Old English has been somewhat overstated in the past. Three Old English riddles show the direct influence of Symphosius (45, 81, 82); two are translations from the Latin of Aldhelm (33, 38). Elsewhere (for example, in 14, 24, 36, 49, 58, 61, 68, 79, 80, 84) riddle subjects and motifs may be the same, but this could be caused by similar perceptions or a common nonriddlic source such as the natural lore of Pliny or Isidore. And in the case of Anglo-Latin writers, it is often impossible to say of comparative Latin and English passages, which was the likely source and which the derivative.

The Latin riddles are exercises in ingenuity. Each offers its solution in a title, then turns on a simple metaphor or paradox like a small jewel set with wit. The Latin riddles parade without play. They lack the imaginative power which allows the poet to sense, sing, and celebrate the nonhuman world about him. The Old English riddles are projective play. They expand the self and inspire the world (whether bird, shield, bookworm, or storm) with lyrical power. They play with mystery. Consider, for example, the comparative anchors of Symphosius and the Old English riddler:

Anchor

My twin points are bound by an iron bar.
I wrestle with wind, struggle with the sea.
I probe deep waters—I bite the earth.
—Symphosius[13]

*   *   *

In battle I rage against wave and wind,
Strive against storm, dive down seeking
A strange homeland, shrouded by the sea.
In the grip of war, I am strong when still;
In battle-rush, rolled and ripped
In flight. Conspiring wind and wave
Would steal my treasure, strip my hold,

13. All translations of medieval Latin riddles are my own. The originals may be found in volumes 133 and 133A of the *Corpus Christianorum Series Latina* (Turnhout: Brepols, 1968). The anchor riddle of Symphosius quoted here is from vol. 133A, p. 682.

But I seize glory with a guardian tail
As the clutch of stones stands hard
Against my strength. Can you guess my name?
—Old English Riddle 14

The Latin riddle is a quick succession of controlled steps. The title gives us the solution; the riddle is a rhetorical show. First we have the creature's shape and composition, next the metaphor of anchor as wave-warrior, finally the paradox of sea-diver and earth-biter. The "I" of the riddle is never in doubt—it is the poet's plain pretense. The "I" of the Old English riddle is unknown, but as the metaphor of the storm-warrior unfolds in lyrical beauty, the eye of the solver is opened to the clutch and roll of the anchor's war-world. Here the eye/I of the creature draws us in to sustained belief. We rage and struggle, seek a shrouded home, battle the wind- and wave-thieves for a clutch of glory and the ship's hold. The treasure of this riddle is its liberative power: it draws us from the bone-house into an iron body and a battle-storm. We have never been in this imaginative world before—it is a dreamlike mirror of our own war-world. The mind rolls, the anchor glories—it is a strange and heartening synchronicity. What we guess finally is what we have become. There is nothing like this in the Latin of Symphosius.

The Latin inkhorn riddle of Eusebius turns on the contrast between present bitterness and past glory, but the contrast is carried to a new elegiac power in the haunting lament of the Old English horn:

Inkhorn

Once a fateful weapon, I rode with the arms
Of the bull, a bold-riding battle-crest.
Now my carved belly holds a bitter drink
Though my belch seems bright, sweet, clean.
—Eusebius[14]

*　　*　　*

We stood, tall hard twins, my brother
And I—pointed and perched on a homeland
Higher and nobler for our fierce adorning.

14. *Corpus Christianorum Series Latina*, 133: 240.

Often the forest, dear sheltering wood,
Was our night-cover, rain-shield for creatures
Shaped by God. Now grim usurpers
Must steal our homeland glory, hard young
Brothers who press in our place. Parted,
We suffer separate sorrows. In my belly
Is a black wonder—I stand on wood.
Untwinned I guard the table's end.
What hoard holds my lost brother in the wide
World I will never know. Once we rode
The high side of battle, hard warriors
Keeping courage together—neither rushed
To the fray alone. Now unwhole creatures
Tear at my belly. I cannot flee.
The man who follows my tracks of glory
For wealth and power, in a different light
May find what is wholly for his soul's delight.
                              —Old English Riddle 84

The Latin creature moves wittily from the bull's battle-crest to a clean belch of wisdom. The clever manipulation calls attention to the poet as manipulator. The voice of the horn is not embodied. Nothing in the language compels us to ride from head to table or to taste the bitter drink. Nothing in the riddle breathes *I am*. The Old English horn creates in its (his) elegiac cry the fierce consciousness of human suffering. The horn-warrior laments a lost, glorious homeland and suffers separation from his twin brother. In his unstable mind history reweaves itself as nightmare—recollection only increases his anxiety and pain. His fate is hard—he guards in his belly a bitter, black treasure which the unwhole quill-birds attack. Even harder is not knowing his brother's fate. Isolated on the board, surrounded by enemies, he is tormented by uncertain memory and by doubts about the nature of fate in an unstable world. Ironically he finds consolation "in a different light" by the end of the poem—the tracks from his belly (in this light *his* tracks) may lead men through letters to wisdom and deep delight. Isolation, suffering, lament for youthful glories and lost kin, recollection turning to nightmare, the progress from melancholy to wisdom—these are some of the characteristics of Old English elegiac poems like "The Wanderer" and "The Wife's Lament."[15] Certainly the seeds (or perhaps the hybrid blooms) of this tradition are present in the horn riddle. Unlike the Latin effort, this riddle hauls us into the landscape of suffering and forces us to feel with the creature doubt and pain. The poem calls forth our powers of recognition and realization as the Latin riddle does not. This is a more subtle shaping typical of the Old English riddles. The Latin horn is always a creature outside, an *other* manipulated by the poet. The Anglo-Saxon horn in its warlike suffering and sorrow is simply one of us. When we discover his plight, we discover ourselves.

Like the Latin riddles, learned dialogues may have influenced and been influenced by the Exeter Book riddles. In *The Dark Ages*, W. P. Ker calls riddles and dialogues "common forms of instruction and literary entertainment which have a large influence on the culture of the Middle Ages."[16] Of the dialogue he says:

> [It] supplied two common rhetorical wants. It was a sort of rhetorical catechism, or a dictionary of poetical synonyms and periphrases, —varieties of *kenning*, to use the convenient and intelligible Norse name. It might also be the frame of a collection of riddles, which were a favourite exercise for fancy and rhetorical skill combined.[17]

The use of riddles (or riddlic metaphors) as an important rhetorical device in medieval dialogue may be seen in Alcuin's eighth-century Latin "Dialogue with Pippin" and in the ninth- or tenth-century Old English dialogue poem, "Solomon and Saturn." Alcuin was an English churchman, a writer of riddles, master of the York school, and in the late eighth century,

15. For the characteristics of the Old English elegy, see B. J. Timmer, "The Elegiac Mood in Old English Poetry," *English Studies* 24 (1942): 34–36; R. F. Leslie, *Three Old English Elegies* (Manchester: Manchester University Press, 1961); S. B. Greenfield, "The Old English Elegies," in *Continuations and Beginnings*, ed. E. G. Stanley (London: Thomas Nelson, 1966), pp. 142–75; and Rosemary Woolf, "*The Wanderer, The Seafarer*, and the Genre of *Planctus*," in *Anglo-Saxon Poetry: Essays in Appreciation*, ed. L. E. Nicholson and D. W. Frese (Notre Dame, Ind.: University of Notre Dame Press, 1975), pp. 192–207. Some of my observations on the elegiac horn riddle were first made in formal response to a paper on the same subject by Edith Williams at a special session of the 1978 Modern Language Association meeting. The session devoted to Old English riddles was organized by Tim Lally.

16. W. P. Ker, *The Dark Ages* (New York: Charles Scribner's Sons, 1904), p. 86.

17. Ibid., p. 87.

Charlemagne's principal educator and head of his palace school at Archen. Alcuin's "Dialogue with Pippin" (Pippin was a son of Charlemagne) shows how the occasional metaphoric play of medieval dialogue could become riddlic. The scholar questions and the boy answers:

What is sleep?—The image of death.
What is man's liberty?—Innocence.
What is the head?—The crown of the body.
What is the body?—The home of the mind.

. . . .

What is the mouth?—The nourisher of the body.
What are the teeth?—The millstones of our food.
What are the lips?—The doors of the mouth.
What is the throat?—The devourer of the food.
What are the hands?—The workmen of the body.

. . . .

What is the moon?—The eye of night; the giver of dew; the
   prophetess of the weather.
What are the stars?—The paintings of the summit of nature; the
   seaman's pilots; the ornaments of night.
What is rain?—The earth's conception; the mother of corn.
What is a cloud?—The night of day; the labour of the eyes.
What is wind?—The perturbation of air; the moving principle of
   water; the dryer of earth.
What is earth?—The mother of the growing; the nurse of the
   living; the storehouse of life; the devourer of all things.

. . . .

What is a wonder?—I saw a man standing; a dead man walking
   who never existed.
How could this be?—An image in water.

. . . .

An unknown person without tongue or voice spoke to me, who
   never existed before, nor has existed since, nor ever will be again:
   and whom I neither heard nor knew.—It was your dream.
I saw the dead produce the living, and by the breath of the living
   the dead were consumed.—From the friction of [sticks] fire was
   produced, which consumed.

. . . .

A Feast of Creatures

Who is he that will rise higher if you take away his head?—Look
at your bed and you will find him there.

. . . .

I saw a flying woman with an iron beak, a wooden body, and a
feathered tail, carrying death.—She is a companion of soldiers.
[What is a soldier?—A wall of power, the dread of an enemy, a
glorious service.]
What is that which is, and is not?—Nothing.
How can a thing be, yet not exist?—In name and not in fact.
What is a silent messenger?—That which I hold in my hand.
What is that?—My letter.[18]

The dialogue begins with plain questions and simple metaphoric answers.
When the talk turns to cosmology, the metaphors spin out—answers imi-
tating riddles. What is the eye of night, the giver of dew, the prophetess
of weather? The moon. When Alcuin asks, "What is a wonder?" (in the
Old English riddles the creature is often a "wonder" or "marvel"), Pippin
responds with a true riddle. From that point on the exchange is entirely
in riddles—ranging from the slightly bawdy bedroom wonder (probably a
pillow) to the philosophical paradox of the apparently real nothing. The
dialogue thus becomes a seed-frame for riddles.

The Old English "Solomon and Saturn" is a ninth- or tenth-century
poetic dialogue in two parts. In the first part the pre-Christian Saturn,
"prince of the Chaldeans," asks a series of questions about the Pater Noster
to which Solomon replies in the light of Christian doctrine. The second
and longer section of the poem is a riddlelike dialogue on the nature of the
world and the shape of creation. Here the questions are sometimes deeply
riddlic and may have been influenced by the form and style of the earlier
Exeter Book riddles. Two examples may suffice:

Saturn said:

What dumb creature rests in its den
Wise and silent with seven tongues,

18. "Disputation regalis et nobilissimi iuvenio Pippini cum Albino scholastico," lines 17–20,
28–32, 51–56, 86–87, 90–91, 101, 104–9. For the Latin text, see Walther Suchier, ed., *Illinois
Studies in Language and Literature*, vol. 24, pt. 2, pp. 137–43. The translation quoted is by
Sharon Turner (except for bracketed material, which is my own translation) and appears in
The History of the Anglo-Saxons (London: Longman, 1852), 3: 380–82.

Each tongue pointed with twenty blades,
Each blade an angel's wisdom that can raise
The gold walls of Jerusalem and cause
The red rood of Christ, the glory-cross,
The truth-sign to shine? Say what I mean.

Solomon said:

Books are bound with glory—they bode
Good counsel and conscious will.
They are man's strength and firm foundation,
His anchored thought. They lift the mind
From melancholy and help hard need.

. . . .

Saturn said:

What creature walks the world shaking
Its firm foundations, waking sorrow
Like a grim wanderer. No star or stone,
Water or wild beast escapes its grip;
Things great and small, hard and soft,
Submit—it feasts on ground-walkers,
Sky-floaters, sea-swimmers in thousands.

Solomon said:

Age is an earth-warrior with power over all;
In its chains all struggle, in its prison keep.
Working its will, it crushes tree,
Rips twig, whips the standing ship
In the water, beats it to the ground.
It jaws birds, death-wrestles wolves,
Outlasts stones. It slays steel,
Bites iron with rust, and takes us too.[19]

In his introduction to "Solomon and Saturn," Dobbie notes that the riddling questions and answers of the poem are much in the style of the Old Norse *Vafthruthnismal* in which Odin and the giant Vafthruthnir

19. "Solomon and Saturn," ll. 230–42, 283–301; *ASPR*, 6: 39–41. In the initial exchange the book with seven tongues is probably the book with seven seals in Revelation. The blades are presumably sharp-edged pages.

engage in a riddlelike contest of wits.[20] The questions in the Norse poem are often cosmological and the answers riddles wrapped in myth. For example:

> "What is the horse called that draws up day
>   Each morning for mankind?"

> "The sky-horse is Skinfaxi, Shining-mane,
>   Who draws the glittering day.
> The greatest of horses to all heroes—
>   His mane is a bright flame."

>   .   .   .   .

> "What is the source of wind that wanders
>   The waves unseen?"

> "The Corpse-Eater Hraesvelg sits in the skin
>   Of an eagle at the end of heaven.
> When his wings beat, wind moves
>   Over the world of men."[21]

A similar riddle contest takes place in the Icelandic *Heidreks Saga* (sometimes known as the *Hervarar Saga*) where Odin in the disguise of an old man, Gestumblindi, matches wits with the proud persecutor, King Heidrek. Gestumblindi, accused of crimes, tries to escape royal judgment by stumping the king with a riddle. The disguised god riddles while the king answers:

> "What strange marvel
> did I see without,
> in front of Delling's door;
> two things lifeless,
> twain unbreathing,

20. *ASPR*, 6: lv.

21. *Vafthruthnismal*, stanzas 11–12, 36–37 (translation mine). For the original text, see Gustav Neckel, ed., *Edda* (Heidelberg: C. Winter, 1927), pp. 45, 49–50. For a translation of the entire poem, see Henry Adams Bellows, tr., *The Poetic Edda* (New York: Oxford University Press, 1923), pp. 68–83.

were seething a stalk of wounds?
This riddle ponder,
O prince Heidrek!"

"Your riddle is good, Gestumblindi," said the king; "I have
guessed it. Those are smith's bellows; they have no wind unless
they are blown, and they are as lifeless as any other work of smith's
craft, but with them one can as well forge a sword as anything
else."

. . . .

Then said Gestumblindi:

"What is that creature,
a cover to the Danes,
with back gory,
yet guardian of men;
spears it encounters,
to some gives life,
in its hollow hand
a man holds his body?
This riddle ponder,
O prince Heidrek!"

"That is the shield," said the king. "In battles it often becomes
bloody, and it is a good protection for those who are nimble with
it."

. . . .

Then said Gestumblindi:

"Four are hanging,
four are walking,
two point the way out,
two ward the dogs off,
one ever dirty
dangles behind it.

This riddle ponder,
O prince Heidrek!"

"Your riddle is good, Gestumblindi," said the king; "I have guessed it. That is the cow."[22]

Riddlic dialogues like Alcuin's almost certainly took place in the Anglo-Saxon monasteries and in the greater courts as part of the learning process. Whether the game was carried out in the vernacular as "Solomon and Saturn" and the Northern stories suggest is not known—but it seems likely. Elaborate riddle contests are common to a number of cultures and may yet be observed in Britain today.[23]

THE VARIETY OF RIDDLES

The variety of riddles may be analyzed in a number of ways. Charles W. Kennedy, for example, concentrates on the identity of unmasked riddle subjects. He says of the riddles:

> They constitute a mosaic of the actualities of daily experience: a record of man's observing companionship with bird and beast, a listing of the things of which his daily life was woven, the food and drink that assuaged his hunger and thirst, the tools with which he toiled, his instruments of music, and the weapons and armor with which he fought. . . . The range of subjects drawn from Old English life is notable. Among familiar birds we find the cuckoo, hawk, jay, nightingale, owl, swallow, and swan. The animals of country life are represented by the bullock, cock and hen, dog, hedge-hog, ox, sow, badger, wolf. The list of implements and utensils of rustic life is especially wide-ranging, including the bucket, churn, flail, lock and key, loom, millstone, plow, poker, wine-cask, and wagon. Various food stuffs are mentioned, as are

22. *The Saga of King Heidrek the Wise*, ed. and tr. Christopher Tolkien (London: Thomas Nelson, 1960), stanzas 48, 60, 70; pp. 34, 39, 43.
23. See, for example, Kenneth S. Goldstein, "Riddling Traditions in Northeastern Scotland," *Journal of American Folklore* 76 (1962): 330–36.

also ale, beer, mead, and wine. Fishery and the sea are represented by the anchor, boat, fish, oyster, a storm at sea, the wake of a ship. The ever-present threat of violence and war is reflected in the many descriptions of weapons and items of armor: the bow, dagger, helmet, lance, coat of mail, scabbard, shield, sword, and sword-rack.[24]

Kennedy's list of subjects gives us an insight into the scope of riddlic mimesis, but it ignores the literary masks. The record of subjects is real, but the parade of disguises is surreal. The bagpipe is a bird that sings through its foot, the rake scruffs like a dog along walls, the wine-cup sings a seductress's song, and the bookworm is a plundering beast that wolfs down a tribal heritage.[25] Baum classifies riddles according to both subject (e.g., "Natural Phenomena," "Birds," "Music," "Weapons") and technique (e.g., "Chiefly Christian," "Runic," "Obscene"),[26] but the problem with this is that riddles often cross categories. The horn, for example, is both battle-weapon and musical instrument; the magpie is a runically riddled bird; the sun is a heavenly body portrayed as the thane of Christ; and the sword is a weapon that refers obscenely to its phallic double. Also, since the Old English riddles, unlike their Latin cousins, contain no entitled solutions, the hidden subjects change over the years with editorial judgments and shifting critical perceptions. Since 1943, nearly half of Kennedy's solutions have been challenged by various critics.[27]

Whatever the system of subjects, it ought to pose questions about patterns of inclusion. Tools and weapons, instruments of writing and song, animals and birds, heavenly bodies, church-related objects—these are not surprising riddle subjects for the Anglo-Saxons. But why so many birds, so few animals, and no bugs? Where are the traditional Anglo-Saxon "beasts of battle" of the heroic poems—the eagle, raven, and wolf? Why only the domesticated ox and wild fox from the animal world? Where are the dog,

24. Charles W. Kennedy, *The Earliest English Poetry* (New York: Oxford University Press, 1943), p. 134.

25. The French surrealists actually played a riddlic game of disguises called by Breton "One in the Other." See Roger Callois's description of this in "Riddles and Images," tr. Jeffrey Mehlman, *Yale French Studies* 41 (1968): 148–58.

26. Baum, *Anglo-Saxon Riddles of the Exeter Book*.

27. Critical debate on each riddle is summarized in my text edition.

goat, deer, and pig? Where are the plants that play such an important part in the medical writings and charms? Why so many ships and no wagon? (Roman roads were falling into disrepair and English rivers, more navigable than their modern counterparts, were regularly used for commercial and personal travel.) Why are tools riddled so often, people so rarely? (Normally people are part of the disguise.) Why Lot and the one-eyed seller of garlic alone among men? Must one be physically or psychically monstrous to be riddled? Why are human abstractions such as *lof and dom* (praise and glory), love and death, good and evil—so important elsewhere in the poetry —never riddled? By asking such questions, we may come to discover in the system of solutions a useful set of keys to Anglo-Saxon culture.

In the fields of folklore and anthropology, riddles are normally classified not according to their solutions but according to their descriptive motifs. This system of classification was proposed by Robert Lehmann-Nitsche[28] and elaborated by Archer Taylor.[29] Creatures in primarily metaphoric riddles are grouped according to their disguises. Creatures disguised as humans, for example, occupy one class; those disguised as animals another. A creature compared to a variety of things (man, animal, plant, object) occupies a different class, as does a creature linked with an erotic double. Since oral riddles are often shorter and simpler than literary riddles, they are more easily classified in this way; but the system may be used to chart the general typology of riddlic descriptions in Old English. The outline below is a modified form of the anthropological model with examples from the Old English riddles:[30]

1. *Biomorphic group.* The riddle subject is compared to a living creature, but it is difficult to tell whether the creature's disguise is a person, animal, or plant. So the iceberg (66) lives and moves and is paradoxically bone-water, but whether she is disguised as sea plant, crustacean, miraculous

28. Robert Lehmann-Nitsche, "Zur Volkskunde Argentiniens, I: Rätsel," *Zeitschrift des Vereins für Volkskunde* 24 (1914): 240–55.
29. Archer Taylor, *English Riddles from Oral Tradition* (Berkeley and Los Angeles: University of California Press, 1951).
30. My categories are based on those of Lehmann-Nitsche, Taylor, and also Charles Scott, who discusses riddle classification systems in "Some Approaches to the Study of the Riddle," in *Studies in Language, Literature, and Culture of the Middle Ages and Later*, ed. E. Bagby Atwood and Archibald Hill (Austin, Tex.: University of Texas Press, 1969), pp. 111–27.

mermaid, or fish is difficult to tell. The bellows (83) is alive and animate with belly and eye, but its exact disguise is undiscoverable.

2. *Zoomorphic group.* The subject is compared to an animal. The rake (32) "scruffs walls / Or drags fields for plunder." And the bagpipe's "shape is strange, / Her beak hung down, her hands and feet / Slung up like a shouldered bird" (29).

3. *Anthropomorphic group.* The subject is compared to a person. This is the most common comparison in the Old English riddles. The shield (3) is a warrior, the nightingale (6) an evening-poet, the cuckoo (7) an orphan, the wine-cup (9) an alluring lady, the iceberg (31) a witch-warrior, mead (25) a wrestler, the inkhorn (84) a separated twin, and so on. The non-human subject taking human disguise is an implicit part of nearly every riddle.

4. *Phytomorphic group.* The subject is compared to a plant. This is an uncommon form in Old English except where objects were in fact initially plants such as the tree turned ram (51) or spear (71), and the reed turned pen (58). The phallus is linked with the onion (23) as part of an erotic riddle (see below), but together they share a vaguely biomorphic disguise.

5. *Inanimate object group.* The subject is compared to an inanimate object. The sword (69) is a treasure, the chalice (57) a gold ring; the river (81) is a house for fish. Certain erotic riddles (see below) utilize inanimate disguises: the helmet and vagina (59) are closely guarded treasures, and the sexual churn (59) is filled with a butter-baby!

6. *Multiple comparison group.* The subject is compared to a variety of things. The tree of riddle 28 is bloom, blaze, traveler, and cross (or cup). The magpie (22) can "bark like a dog, bleat like a goat, / Honk like a goose, shriek like a hawk." The creation riddle (38) is a catalogue of comparative delights—for example:

> I am harder and colder than the bitter frost,
> The sword of morning that falls on the ground.
> I am hotter than Vulcan's flickering fire,
> Sweeter than bee-bread laced with honey,
> Galled as wormwood gray in the forest.
> I can gorge like an old giant—bloated,
> Bellied—or live sustained without food.

7. *Selected details group.* The riddle enumerates descriptive details, typically of the creature's form or function—in either positive or negative fashion. The uncertain creature of riddle 26 is:

> . . . felled, cut, carved,
> Bleached, scrubbed, softened, shaped,
> Twisted, rubbed, dried, adorned,
> Bound, and borne off to the doorways of men.

Another mystery creature (37) seems to function in lively fashion without the necessary prerequisites:

> It has no hands or feet
> To touch the ground, no mouth to speak
> With men or mind to know the books
> Which claim it is the least of creatures
> Shaped by nature. It has no soul, no life,
> Yet it moves everywhere in the wide world.
> It has no blood or bone, yet carries comfort
> To the children of men on middle-earth.

The details are often selected to produce an implicit sense of paradox and to undermine any consistent sense of disguise.

8. *Neck-riddle group.* Taylor explains the appellation: "Another very curious variety of enigma consists in a description of a scene that can be interpreted only by the one who sets the puzzle. The terms used are not confusing, but the situation itself seems inexplicable. In many northern European versions of such puzzles the speaker saves his neck by the riddle, for the judge or executioner has promised release in exchange for a riddle that cannot be guessed."[31] The one-eyed seller of garlic (82) is a neck-riddle whose answer we know only because it is derived from the Latin riddle of Symphosius whose answer is passed along in its title.

31. Archer Taylor, "The Varieties of Riddles," in *Philologica: The Malone Anniversary Studies*, ed. Thomas A. Kirby and Henry Bosley Woolf (Baltimore, Md.: Johns Hopkins University Press, 1949), p. 6.

9. *Arithmetical group*. The subject's form or function is described as an arithmetical puzzle. Strictly speaking, there are no exclusively arithmetical riddles in the collection, but several of the riddles have arithmetical parts. The ship of riddle 34, for example, has "Four feet under belly, eight on its back, / Two wings, twelve eyes, six heads, one track," and the one-eyed seller of garlic (82) has "one eye, / Two feet, twelve hundred heads, / A back and belly—two hands, arms, / Shoulders—one neck, two sides."

10. *Family relation group*. The subject is described primarily in terms of its family relations—often with a bizarre twist. The riddle about Lot and his family (44) falls into this category. Because of Lot's incest, his daughters are also his wives, their sons his sons (and grandsons!), each son an uncle and nephew to the other. Elsewhere in the riddles, family relations are often part of the metaphoric game: the cuckoo (7) is an adopted orphan, water (80) is the mother of earth-creatures, and the inkhorn (84) is a twin separated from its brother.

11. *Cryptomorphic group*. The solution is somehow coded and concealed in the riddle. In Old English this is done with runes or letters in the following riddles: 17, 22, 40, 62, and 73.

12. *Homonymic group*. The solution turns on a homonym. The one example of this is riddle 88 where the solution, Old English *boc*, means both "beech" and "book."

13. *Erotic group*. The erotic double-entendre riddle has both a prim and a pornographic solution. This places the potential solver in a double bind: either his naiveté or his salacious imagination is bound to be exposed. Old English riddles in this genre are 23, 35, 42, 43, 52, 59, and 60. Erotic elements, but without the sustained sense of double entendre, also occur in 10, 18, 40, 61, and 87.

14. *Tricky question group*. Often included in folkloristic categories are not-quite riddles called *joking questions* ("What happens to little girls who swallow bullets?" "Their hair grows out in bangs"); *wisdom questions* ("What is whiter than milk?" "Snow" and "What is blacker than a crow?" "Its feathers"); *puzzles* ("If a chicken and a half could lay an egg and a half in a day and a half, how long would it take five chickens to lay five eggs?" "One day"); and *riddle parodies* ("What is big, gray, lives in trees,

and is dangerous?" "An elephant—I lied about the trees"). Tricky questions rarely form the basis of literary riddles; there are no Old English riddles in this category.[32]

As with the previous classification systems, sometimes an Old English riddle falls into more than one group. The *magpie* riddle (22) is cryptomorphic—it also contains multiple comparisons. The onion (23) is erotic —it also seems to cross categories in a biomorphic way (the creature is rooted, shaggy, and a gallant help to women). The one-eyed seller of garlic (82) is a kind of arithmetical neck-riddle. Even so the categories are useful in characterizing most riddle descriptions and in isolating the major riddlic modes. The Anglo-Saxons seem to favor the anthropomorphic mode and to shy away from human solution-subjects. The most common riddlic game is to give something nonhuman a human disguise—thus the reed is a messenger, the ram a warrior, mead a wrestler, the moon a wanderer, and the inkhorn a separated twin. This metaphoric movement carries us out into the Other where we find an image of the self. We escape in the body of wine to find a female temptress. We arch into bow to become a belly laced with slaughter. We hide in the pouch of the bee only to wrestle (as mead) with the mind of man.

Another traditional way of characterizing riddles is according to the narrative stance of each. In some riddles the riddler recounts a "strange wonder"; in some the creature itself sings. The riddles may be divided into projective and nonprojective types. Nonprojective riddles may be further divided into eyewitness riddles (which often begin with the formula, *I saw a creature*), hearsay riddles (which often begin with the formula, *I heard of a creature*), and purely descriptive riddles which begin without reference to the riddler.[33] Examples of nonprojective riddles may be seen in the

---

32. For more on the folk traditions of not-quite-riddles, see Roger D. Abrahams and Alan Dundes, "Riddles," in *Folklore and Folklife: An Introduction*, ed. Richard M. Dorson (Chicago: University of Chicago Press, 1972), pp. 129–43. The examples quoted are taken from this article.

33. Most editors and many critics have remarked on the different voices of the riddles. The terms "projective" and "nonprojective" are my own. I take the terms "hearsay" and "eyewitness" from Ann Harleman Stewart, "Old English Riddle 47 as Stylistic Parody," *Papers on Language and Literature* 11 (1975): 227–41.

openings of the bellows (eyewitness), bread (hearsay), and ox (descriptive) riddles:

I saw a creature with a strange belly
Huge and swollen, handled by a servant,
Hard-muscled and hand-strong, a mighty man.

* * *

I heard of something rising in a corner,
Swelling and standing up, lifting its cover.

* * *

This strange creature, a stripling boy,
Sought sweet pleasure pumping joy.
His nourishing Bess gave him four
White fountains—murmur and roar.

Nonprojective riddles (which constitute half the corpus) often end with some variation of the riddler's taunt, "Say what I mean."

In projective riddles the narrative voice is the voice of the creature quickened by the poetic imagination. Projective riddles often begin with the formula, *I am* or *I was*. The nightingale in riddle 6, for example, sings:

I am a mimic with many tongues,
Warbling tunes, shifting tones,
Jugging the city with head-song.

And the cuckoo in riddle 7 recalls its inglorious beginning:

I was an orphan before I was born—
Cast without breath by both parents
Into a world of brittle death, I found
The comfort of kin in a mother not mine.

A Feast of Creatures

Projective riddles often end with a variation of the creature's taunt, "Say who I am."

Thus in half of the riddles the reader identifies with the "I" of the human riddler; in half, with the "I" of the creature. The two narrative stances constitute poles of a perceptual game. Sometimes we escape the bone-house and embody the world; sometimes we see what the world charged with metaphor means. This is an ontological game[34]—the challenge is either, "Say what I mean," or "Say who I am." Meaning depends upon our manipulation in images of the Other. Being paradoxically demands recognition of what Whitman calls the "radical, democratic Me," in the "conservative Not Me, the whole of the material objective universe."[35]

METAPHOR AND RIDDLE

A riddle mediates between man and the Other—its voice is sometimes the bard's, sometimes the bird's. We contrive to know the riddler's meaning, the creature's world. Through other eyes we see our own symbolic systems. With reason we separate day from night, man from monster, plant from penis—only to discover in riddles a nightmare of resemblances and crossed

34. For more on poetry as ontology, see John Crowe Ransom, *The World's Body* (New York: Charles Scribner's Sons, 1938), and *The New Criticism* (New York: New Directions, 1941). On the "ontological function of metaphor," see Karsten Harries, "Metaphor and Transcendence," *Critical Inquiry* 5 (1978): 73–90.

35. Walt Whitman, *Specimen Days*, vol. 1 of *Prose Works 1892*, ed. Floyd Stovall (New York: New York University Press, 1963), p. 258. The quotation in full is:

> The most profound theme that can occupy the mind of man—the problem on whose solution science, art, the bases and pursuits of nations, and everything else, including intelligent human happiness, (here to-day, 1882, New York, Texas, California, the same as all times, all lands,) subtly and finally resting, depends for competent outset and argument, is doubtless involved in the query: What is the fusing explanation and tie—what the relation between the (radical, democratic) Me, the human identity of understanding, emotions, spirit, &c., on the one side, of and with the (conservative) Not Me, the whole of the material objective universe and laws, with what is behind them in time and space, on the other side?

The passage is cited in Giles Gunn, *The Interpretation of Otherness* (New York: Oxford University Press, 1979), p. 175.

categories. Can the fox be a great mother, the moon a night-bandit, the sword a celibate and serving thane? Can the dead ox revive to carry man (shoes) or sing through its skin the word of God (Bible)? Can a bird be a poet, a bagpipe a bird? This is the power the word confers—especially in the shape of metaphor.[36]

Disguise and disclosure are the twin movements of metaphor and riddle. Aristotle discovered the poles of the dance. In discussing riddles and metaphors in *The Poetics* and *Rhetoric*, he says:

> Good metaphors can usually be made from successful riddles, for metaphors are a kind of riddle.[37]

> The essence of a riddle is to express facts by combining them in an impossible way; this cannot be done by the mere arrangement of words but requires the use of metaphor.[38]

> Most felicitous sayings rely on metaphor and on a capacity to deceive beforehand. We have even more obviously learned something if things are the opposite of what we thought they were, and the mind seems to say to itself: "How true; I was mistaken." . . . Good riddles delight us for the same reason, for we learn something from them, and they are in the form of metaphors.[39]

Riddles and metaphors disguise one creature in the garb of another. The bird is a poet, the blade is a warrior, the rake is a dog. The real creature is what I. A. Richards calls the *tenor*, the disguise is the *vehicle;* the common *ground* is what makes the comparison, the disguise possible.[40] The nightingale and poet sing and celebrate beauty, the blade and warrior

36. My discussion of metaphor is based on a number of sources—primarily the *Poetics* of Aristotle, I. A. Richards's *The Philosophy of Rhetoric* (New York: Oxford University Press, 1936), much of Claude Lévi-Strauss's work on metaphoric systems (see for example *Totemism*, tr. Rodney Needham [Boston: Beacon Press, 1963] and *The Savage Mind* [Chicago: University of Chicago Press, 1966]), the recent work of Maranda and Stewart (see articles listed in Selected Bibliography), and my graduate work in anthropology in a course on "The Ethnography of Symbolic Forms," taught by J. David Sapir (University of Pennsylvania, 1969).

37. Aristotle, *Rhetoric* 1405b; *On Poetry and Style*, tr. G. M. A. Grube (Indianapolis, Ind.: Bobbs-Merrill Co., 1958), p. 71.

38. Ibid., *Poetics* 1458a; *On Poetry and Style*, p. 47.

39. Ibid., *Rhetoric* 1412a; *On Poetry and Style*, p. 94.

40. Richards, *The Philosophy of Rhetoric*, especially chaps. 5 and 6.

serve and slay, the rake and dog scruff along the ground. In addition to Richards's triad of terms, there is also what I call the *gap*, those characteristics which separate the true tenor from the vehicle, the real creature from the assumed disguise.[41] By calling the nightingale "bright singer of beauty," we highlight the connection between bard and bird (the ground). By calling the bird a "winged, penless poet," we highlight the distinction (the gap). Ground words reinforce the metaphoric equation; gap words recall the separate worlds of tenor and vehicle. The ground extends a metaphor; the gap produces paradox. An extended image often contains both ground and gap. For example, the rake as dog might be "a one-legged ground-scruffer," the blade as warrior, "a gray battle-thane," or gold as a tyrant, "a bright-cloaked, hammered king." The gap and ground produce the clash and confirmation of metaphor, the collision and collusion of worlds.[42]

How does this work in practice in the Old English riddles? The lyre (tenor) is disguised as a lady singer (vehicle):

> She shapes for her listeners a haunting sound
> Who sings through her sides. Her neck is round
> And delicately shaped; on her shoulders draped,
> Beautiful jewels.

The tenor is hidden, the vehicle highlighted. The ground is plain—both a lady and a lyre may have lovely round necks, may make music for their audiences, may have shoulders decked with beautiful jewels. The gap gives pause—this lady sings through her sides (and the roundness of neck may point more to shape and artisan's craft than statuesque beauty). The metaphor is spun out into a lyrical conceit. The ground gives good reason for the spinning; the gap produces a paradox and gives us a clue.

41. My "metaphoric gap" corresponds in some ways to the oppositional or contradictive elements of riddles identified by Robert A. Georges and Alan Dundes in "Toward a Structural Definition of the Riddle," *Journal of American Folklore* 76 (1963): 111–18.

42. The "collision" and "collusion" functions of poetic imagery were first mentioned by C. Day Lewis in *The Poetic Image* (London: Jonathan Cape, 1947), p. 72; the functions are also discussed by Harries in "Metaphor and Transcendence," *Critical Inquiry* 5 (1978): 73. Two works on the theory of metaphor are most useful: the "Special Issue on Metaphor" of *Critical Inquiry* 5 (1978) and Paul Ricoeur's *The Rule of Metaphor*, tr. Robert Czerny et al. (Toronto: University of Toronto Press, 1977).

Sometimes the gap seems like a chasm from which reality will never be retrieved, as in riddle 7:

> I was an orphan before I was born—
> Cast without breath by both parents
> Into a world of brittle death, I found
> The comfort of kin in a mother not mine.

Our sense of logical possibility is constantly assaulted. An orphan is a child. A child must have been born. The sign of a successful birthing is breath. The world of welcome is not that of the dead but the living. The mother of comfort who bears the child must be kin. But the child is a bird, in this case a cuckoo. It is born breathless in an egg, deposited in animated death into the nest of the host mother where it hatches and is nurtured by its foster-mother (at some expense to her own brood). The metaphoric leap predisposes us to a human perception of the riddlic terms. But the bird is and is not one of us.

Sometimes a clashing of metaphors creates the gap, as in the case of the riddlic moon:

> I saw a wonderful creature carrying
> Light plunder between its horns.
> Curved lamp of the air, cunningly formed,
> It fetched home its booty from the day's raid
> And plotted to build in its castle if it could
> A night-chamber brightly adorned.

The moon begins as a horned marauder, perhaps a horn-helmeted Viking or a beast on the hoof. We expect either to plunder, but not to plunder *light*. Then the moon turns metaphorically into a curved lamp. Paradoxically it produces what it steals—light.[43] It carries a treasure and is trea-

43. The light carried between the horns of the nearly new moon is actually earthlight, sunlight reflected from earth to moon, what the ballad, "Sir Patrick Spens" calls the "new moon late yestreen / Wi' the auld moon in her arm." The Anglo-Saxons had no cosmological terms for the phenomenon—indeed it appears to have been unrecognized apart from the central metaphor of this riddle. So as Harries says, "What metaphor names may transcend human understanding so that our language cannot capture it" ("Metaphor and Transcen-

sure. In each metaphor a gap provides a clue to the context of the creature and points to the true solution: the marauder's treasure is light; the lamp is a rider of the air. The clash of metaphors also produces a gap. How can a horned creature also be an air-rider and bright lamp? Then the lamp turns plotter and bedroom builder as the metaphoric mode becomes increasingly anthropomorphic. This conceit is spun out as the warrior sun arrives to reclaim its rightful light and drive the plundering plotter off into morning.

In Old English poetry the kernel form of riddlic metaphor is the kenning, a Nordic device for calling something by a name it is not, then modifying it with a contextual clue.[44] Examples of kennings include bone-house (body), battle-light (sword), heaven's candle (sun), sea-horse (ship), whale's road (sea), and battle-snake (arrow). In each case the tenor is hidden in riddlelike fashion and the vehicle appears as the second element of the compound, the gap (presenting a paradox and giving a contextual clue) as the first element. The two terms of the kenning make up part of the analogy inherent in metaphor according to Aristotle,[45] so that, for example:

$$\frac{body}{bone} \ldots \frac{house}{strut}$$

and

$$\frac{sword}{battle} \ldots \frac{light}{hall}$$

dence," p. 74). Metaphor has often paved the way to scientific discovery. W. V. Quine notes that "metaphor . . . flourishes in playful prose and high poetical art, but it is vital also at the growing edges of science and philosophy" ("Afterthoughts on Metaphor," *Critical Inquiry* 5 [1978]: 161).

44. The relationship between riddle and kenning has oft been noted. See, for example: Ker, *The Dark Ages*, p. 87; Tupper, *The Riddles of the Exeter Book*, p. xiv; Johan Huizinga, *Homo Ludens: A Study of the Play Element in Culture* (Boston: Beacon Press, 1955), pp. 134–35; Northrop Frye, *Anatomy of Criticism* (Princeton: Princeton University Press, 1957), p. 280; Agop Hacikyan, *A Linguistic and Literary Analysis of Old English Riddles* (Montreal: Cassalini, 1966), pp. 34 ff.; Andrew Welsh, *Roots of Lyric* (Princeton: Princeton University Press, 1978), pp. 36 ff. The fullest discussion of the relationship is Ann Harleman Stewart, "Kenning and Riddle in Old English," *Papers in Language and Literature* 15 (1979): 115–36.

45. Aristotle, *Poetics* 1457b; *On Poetry and Style*, p. 45.

In each case the analogy may generate four separate kennings, each a miniature metaphoric riddle. The kennings are:

1. bone-house (body)
2. body-strut (bone)
3. strutted body (house)
4. house-bone (strut)

1. battle-light (sword)
2. sword-hall (battle)
3. hall-sword (light)
4. light-battle (hall)

Each of the kennings could be spun out into a riddle. For example, we might take *bone* as our solution, and using the metaphor of the body-strut begin:

> I am the strut and strength of body,
> The unnailed timber of a living house.
> I hold flesh, shield lungs, stiffen arms;
> I am brain-hoard and hand-shape,
> Unknown to the talking and rising tongues.

The riddle spins out the principle of the kenning. Call the creature something it is not. Modify the calling by a catch of contextual truth producing paradox. Metaphorically the bone is a strut, paradoxically a body-strut; metaphorically a timber, paradoxically unnailed. The list of attributes reinforces the real bodily context, but the creature claims to be curiously absent from two tongues (the second of which is the seed of another riddle). By solving the riddle we raise to consciousness not only the bone but the set of kennings implicit in the central metaphor. We discover not only body-strut but house-bone.

This analysis of riddle structure gives us an insight into the relationship between Old English riddles and the maxims or gnomic poems. The maxims which occur in two separate collections[46] are a series of statements

46. "Maxims I" (Exeter Maxims), *ASPR*, 3:156–63; "Maxims II" (Cotton Maxims), *ASPR*, 6:55–57.

about the appropriate context, action, or condition of a variety of creatures. The poet of the Cotton maxims ("Maxims II") says, for example:

> The wild hawk shall dwell on the glove,
> The outcast wolf alone in the grove,
> The boar in the wood, tusk-strong.
> A good man seeks glory in his homeland.
> A dagger dwells in the hand, gold-stained.
> A gem rides the ring, broad and tall.
> The stream is wave-bound to mix with the flood.
> The mast stands on a boat, the sail-yard;
> The sword on a breast, ancient iron.
> The dragon dwells in the cave of jewels,
> Old and proud. The fish spawns its kind
> In the water. The king deals rings in the hall.[47]

Each creature has its context—a proper place or action. The dragon dwells in the cave, the boar in the wood. A good man seeks homeland glory; a king gives gold rings in the hall. Each contextual pairing constitutes half a kenning. We may complete the kenning by linking two gnomes in a metaphoric equation where the ground makes this appropriate. If the boar in its wood is like the dragon in its cave, then the boar is a wood-dragon and the dragon a cave-boar. Sometimes the linkage is less explicit. The good man may seek glory in his homeland with a dagger as the boar seeks power with his tusks in the wood. A mast may ride on the boat's breast as the sword stands on the breast-deck. And a king's giving of gold rings may be a peculiar form of spawning peace in the hall. The most carefully hidden comparisons (with both ground and gap) make the best kennings, the best miniature riddles. The glove is obviously the hawk's home. But the cave is also the dragon's glove. And the hall is perhaps the king's lair. The wolf is the grove's outlaw; the hawk is a gloved wolf. The dragon is a cave-sword, the sword a hand-dragon—both are ancient and fierce, but one hoards what the other is (treasure). This begins to be a riddle. Sometimes the implicit gnomic connections create their own tensions. For example, the king in his treatment of gold cannot be both cave-dragon and fertile fish. Each gnomic

47. "Maxims II," ll. 17–29; *ASPR*, 6:56.

connection charts a metaphoric world at war with the other—the implied kennings clashing like swords:

$$\frac{king}{hall} :: \frac{dragon}{cave}$$

1. The king is a hall-dragon.
2. The dragon is a cave-king.
3. The hall is the king's cave.
4. The cave is the dragon's hall.

and

$$\frac{king}{gold} :: \frac{fish}{spawn}$$

1. The king is a gold-spawning fish
2. The fish is a spawn-king.
3. Gold is a king's spawn.
4. Spawn is a fish's gold.

Each of these worlds is a separate perception—kingship as nightmare (the Heremod of *Beowulf*) and wish fulfillment (Beowulf himself, a generous king). Each individual gnomic statement puts a creature in a proper, predictable place. We can all agree that a mast stands in a boat and that a good man should at least seek glory. But the placement of gnomes one against another—colluding, colliding—raises the question of perception. It subjectifies reality. It sparks surreal possibilities so that the wooden gnomes begin to alight with a riddlic fire. All's right with the world, the gnomes want to say. But the wrapped riddles cry that the world is filled with unknown shapes. The tension between gnome and riddle, day-reason and nightmare, seems to fire much of Old English poetry. Certainly it is the tension between the sententious Hrothgar and the surreal Grendel which Beowulf is called upon to resolve. And that leads to the question of whether the hero is not a riddle solver spun out in narrative time.

A Feast of Creatures

Riddles have traditionally been considered a minor genre by both folklorists and literary critics.[48] But Aristotle's insight that "good metaphors can usually be made from successful riddles, for metaphors are a kind of riddle,"[49] and his dictum that "we learn above all from metaphors,"[50] constitute an implicit recognition of the importance of riddlic play to the progression of thought. Riddles are common to most primitive cultures.[51] They make a game of probing the normally unconscious categories of perception. They call attention to the arbitrarily shaped and symbolized universe and offer other ways of seeing. The anthropologist Elli Köngäs Maranda says that "riddles make a point of playing with the conceptual borderlines and crossing them for the intellectual pleasure of showing that things are not quite as stable as they appear,"[52] and Ian Hamnett likewise notes that "the ability to construct categories and also to transcend them is central to adaptive learning, and riddles can be seen as a very simple paradigm of how this ability is attained."[53] Recognizing the separate worlds of tenor and vehicle, real creature and assumed disguise, helps us to understand our conceptual categories. Crossing categories by means of riddles helps us to explore the dark corners of our symbolic systems and recharge the related outer and inner landscapes with metaphoric light. What any culture calls monstrous may be simply an unrecognized riddle, an embodied taboo.[54] We place the rake and the dog in separate categorical rooms, but both may be found in the dream-house of toothers, ground-snufflers, and wall-skulkers. In each of us there is an unconscious recognition of other ways of shaping—and this dream-house of uncanny shapes[55] unlocks its doors

48. Charles T. Scott charts some of the reasons for this in "On Defining the Riddle: The Problem of a Structural Unit," *Genre* 2 (1969): 129 ff.

49. Aristotle, *Rhetoric* 1405b; *On Poetry and Style*, p. 71.

50. Ibid., *Rhetoric* 1410b; *On Poetry and Style*, p. 89.

51. Welsh, *Roots of Lyric*, p. 27.

52. Elli Köngäs Maranda, "Theory and Practice of Riddle Analysis," *Journal of American Folklore* 84 (1971): 53.

53. Ian Hamnett, "Ambiguity, Classification and Change: The Function of Riddles," *Man* n.s. 2 (1967): 387.

54. For more on riddle and taboo, see Nigel F. Barley, "Structural Aspects of the Anglo-Saxon Riddle," *Semiotica* 10 (1974): 143–75.

55. According to Freud ("The 'Uncanny,'" in *On Creativity and the Unconscious* [New York: Harper and Row, 1958], pp. 122–61), our sense of the ghastly or uncanny derives from

in our myths and songs, poems and stories. Riddles offer a lyric key to the house of dreams, transforming uncanny creatures into recognizable friends.

Northrop Frye argues that "in archetypal criticism the significant content [of poetry] is the conflict of desire and reality which has for its basis the work of the dream."[56] Poetry may be drawn out in time into narrative romance or suspended in a lyric moment. The poles of poetry are what Aristotle calls *melos* (rhythm, movement, sound) and *opsis* (image, picture, spectacle).[57] Frye argues that the root form of *melos* in lyric poetry is a charm; the root form of *opsis* is a riddle.[58] Both draw the reader into the dream world: the charm is a magical incantation that captures and holds; the riddle a kind of illuminated prison (like a manuscript drawing that catches the eye) which entraps till the key (the true solution) is found.[59]

In Old English poetry, riddles and charms combine elements of *melos* and *opsis:* both share a metaphoric world—both rely upon the yoke of images and reins of sound to draw man into that world. But the motive for metaphor, as Kenneth Burke might say,[60] the strategy, remains distinct. A

---

a childhood desire to project animate power into the surrounding world of inanimate objects. This "omnipotence of thought" leads to the obvious possibilities of nightmarish monsters and talking trees. Freud sees primitive cultures as locked into this childish state of mind—but if this animation is deeply human, as Freud himself suggests, it may be that primitive myths and riddles are a cultural recognition of the process (as is psychoanalysis in the nonprimitive world). Riddles in particular may be a way of raising to consciousness this impulse to animate the world, and by playing with it in a lyric game, of rendering it delightful, acceptable (making the uncanny canny). Thus we recognize and reaffirm that part of the symbolic process which we first used to meet the world. By playing the childish game of riddles, we discover something of our own roots.

56. Frye, *Anatomy*, p. 105.

57. For a discussion of the oral (rhythmic) and visual (patterned) dimensions of literature, see Northrop Frye, "The Archetypes of Literature," *Kenyon Review* 13 (1951), especially pp. 101 ff.; also his *Anatomy of Criticism*, pp. 77 ff. and 278 ff.

58. Frye, *Anatomy*, pp. 278–80. For more on the subject of riddles and charms as roots of lyric poetry, see Welsh, *Roots of Lyric*, chaps. 1, 2, and 6.

59. Frye, *Anatomy*, pp. 278–80; see also his chapter on "Charms and Riddles" in *Spiritus Mundi* (Bloomington, Ind.: Indiana University Press, 1976), pp. 123–47.

60. For "poetry . . . as the adopting of various strategies for the encompassing of situations," see Kenneth Burke, *The Philosophy of Literary Form*, 3d ed. (Berkeley and Los Angeles: University of California Press, 1973), the title essay. For a larger discussion of motive, see *A Grammar of Motives* (Berkeley and Los Angeles: University of California Press, 1969). Motive and metaphor are also treated in *Permanence and Change*, 2d ed. (Indianapolis, Ind.: Bobbs-Merrill Co., 1965).

charm is a strategy for action in a sick or unfruitful world. It is man using metaphor like a knife. A riddle is a matching of wits, a game of disguises. It is man playing with metaphor like a lens. A charmist fears and manipulates the Other. A riddler delights in and dances the Other. A charmist is an operator who wields uncanny shapes below the patient's perception. The riddler plays protagonist as he leads us in to the uncanny world and lends us light. The charmist battles unwilling flesh with the power of the word. He moves through the patient's mind. The riddler shows us our eyes altering, our minds manipulating, our words reshaping that Other world. We move singing through the mind of two. The charmist often chants directions ("Take fennel and boil it with paste and bathe it with egg, then put on the salve";[61] or "Turn three times with the course of the sun, then stretch out and say the litany"[62]), but never challenges, "Say what I mean." His meaning is found in healed flesh, not in the probing and playful mind. He lends us power but leads us to none. In an Old English charm for wens or tumors, the charmist chants:

> Wen, wen, chicken-wen,
> Build no house to enter in,
> No town to hold. Go north, wretch,
> To the neighboring hill where your brother waits
> With a leaf for your head. Under the wolf's paw,
> Under eagle's wing, under eagle's claw,
> May you shrivel like coal in the catch of fire,
> Disappear like dirt on the wall, water in a bucket,
> Tiny as linseed, smaller than a hand-worm's
> Hip-bone, smaller than something that is not![63]

Here there is magical repetition; here there is also metaphor. There is no riddlic projection (the universe is dangerous) but a "speaking to" the creature. Each metaphor is a kind of trap: the wen is caught in its chicken-skin, its wanderer's cloak, its fire-flesh, linseed body, hand-worm's hip-bone. The ground is implicit; there is no gap. If the tenor is lost to the conscious

61. "The Nine Herbs Charm," ll. 68–69; *ASPR*, 6: 121.
62. "For Unfruitful Land," ll. 39–40; *ASPR*, 6: 117.
63. "Against a Wen," *ASPR*, 6: 128.

mind, the word may win. When the creature disappears, we are left with disguises of our own making—over these we have power. How different is the celebration, the lifting to consciousness, the metaphysical greeting of the Other in riddlic play. The charmist uses uncanny shapes to restore the world to its right flesh. The riddler invites us to witness a lyric epiphany as we see the world of our own shaping and realize that flesh is spirit embodied, spirit, symbolizing flesh. Riddlic poetry brings us to this recognition—we shape the Other and in shaping, embody the Self. Without meeting the creature, we are locked in the prison of reified categories and recognized truth. To grow beyond the known we must enter the riddlic world of unrecognizable shapes and make them ours.

RIDDLE AND QUEST

According to Aristotle, metaphor begins with deception and ends with the recognition of a deeper truth. We doubt the riddlic equation: How can a bagpipe be a bird, the shield a warrior, the moon a plunderer, mead a wrestler? But the dreamwork draws us in. We wander a riddlic landscape dimly charted, haunted by unknown or shifting shapes, full of disguised characters, until we reach a kenning,[64] a metaphoric way of knowing that carries us beyond the old categories of perception, beyond the dead world of literal truth. "We have even more obviously learned something if things are the opposite of what we thought they were, and the mind seems to say to itself: 'How true; I was mistaken.' "[65] Bound by our symbols we separate the world into categories: animate/inanimate, subject/object, artifice/artificer, light/dark. Here there is no room for a singing sword, an ox-skin that preaches the Gospel, a quill that tracks culture, and a moth that wolfs songs. Here we do not see that darkness is the owl's light. Like the bird we are blind to the inverse world and must count on metaphor to carry us across. A riddle, a metaphor points to the "thisness of a that, or the thatness of a this."[66] It liberates us from the prison of reified perception and recalls

64. "Kenning" both in the sense of "knowing, understanding" ("to ken" = "to know") and in the sense of "a paraphrastic naming." Both meanings are related to the Old Norse *kenna*, "to perceive, know, make known, name."
65. Aristotle, *Rhetoric* 1412a; *On Poetry and Style,* p. 94.
66. Burke, *Grammar,* p. 503.

A Feast of Creatures

36

the metamorphic flow. It offers us a transverse means of crossing the water, of moving to and from what Whitman calls "the other side" of the universe.[67]

Riddles are common not only to medieval classrooms and modern play-grounds, but to primitive transition rites—courtship contests, weddings, funerals, initiation rites.[68] Often when a man's or a tribe's identity is to be transformed, there are unknown creatures in riddlic guise. The strange world taunts, "Say what I mean," and the solver must discover not only a newly charged world but a newly embodied self. A riddle is a miniature rite of passage, a metaphoric meeting suspended in lyric time. The riddle solver is like a quester entering what Victor Turner calls a liminal world where an old order is suspended and where "monsters startle neophytes into thinking about objects, persons, relationships, and features of their environment they have hitherto taken for granted."[69] The riddle solver moves through the traditional phases of the questing hero:

1. Departure from the dead world of reified categories.

2a. Confrontation with the metaphoric world of unknown monsters and shifting shapes.

2b. Recognition (con-naître = being born with) of the Other and its relation to the Self.

3. Return to the old world with rejuvenative eyes.[70]

The hero's quest in narrative time is the riddle solver's task in the lyric moment—to penetrate the structure of the surreal world, to recognize the uncanny and its relation to the self, to find a solution in the lush world of

67. See the Whitman passage from *Specimen Days* quoted in n. 35.

68. For a summary of the social uses of riddling, see Thomas A. Burns, "Riddling: Occasion to Act," *Journal of American Folklore* 89 (1976): 139–65.

69. Victor Turner, *The Forest of Symbols* (Ithaca, N.Y.: Cornell University Press, 1967), p. 105; for more on liminality, see also Turner's *The Ritual Process* (Chicago: Aldine, 1969).

70. This is a slight modification of the stages proposed by Arnold Van Gennep in *Rites of Passage*, tr. Monika B. Vizedom and Gabriella L. Caffee (Chicago: University of Chicago Press, 1960 [orig. Paris, 1909]). The pattern is best known to students of literature from Joseph Campbell's *The Hero with a Thousand Faces* (Princeton: Princeton University Press, 1949 [Bollingen Series]).

imagery, and to bring back the metaphoric fruit to rejuvenate the dead world.

What sort of monsters inhabit the world of the Old English riddles? A man with one eye and twelve hundred heads, a bird that sings through her dangling foot, a water-witch whose mother is its pregnant daughter, a cock like Christ, and a circle of gold that preaches to men. We even meet an onion and a phallus muscling for attention like twins under a strange riddlic cloak:

> I am a wonderful help to women,
> The hope of something to come. I harm
> No citizen except my slayer.
> Rooted I stand on a high bed.
> I am shaggy below. Sometimes the beautiful
> Peasant's daughter, an eager-armed,
> Proud woman grabs my body,
> Rushes my red skin, holds me hard,
> Claims my head. The curly-haired
> Woman who catches me fast will feel
> Our meeting. Her eye will be wet.

This double-entendre riddle (which may be part of a courting ritual or an attempt to catch the salacious out like a primitive Rorschach test) plays on the notion of crossed categories. The helpmate is rooted like a plant, shaggy like an animal, held like a tool, and stands like a man. Its bed may be covered with blankets or mulch. Its head may be saucy in a strip or a stew. The crossing of categories forces the reader to play the ontological game of venturing with various ideas of order (proposed and discarded solutions, literal and metaphoric truths) into the riddlic world. It forces us to reexamine our perceptual categories and to accept our links with the nonhuman world about us. The riddler not only describes (and jokes about) the phallic onion; he links human sexuality to the green and mythic world of regenerative power. We move from a complacent, predictable way of knowing, through a stage of suspended animation or unknowing, to a deeper, metaphorically embodied way of knowing both phallus and onion. Perhaps we are seduced by the voice itself as it starts with a litany of personal power (the subject "I" four times in five lines) and dissolves into a sensuous and surreal cacophony of parts as the warrior woman (cook or seductress) comes to power. The point is not merely to solve the riddle but to ride the dream-horse home to power. "The real answer to the question implied in a riddle is not a 'thing' outside it, but that which is both word and thing, and is both inside and outside the poem."[71] This is the reader's rite of passage—separation from the world of generally accepted ideas of order, transition through an unknown, metaphoric and mythic world populated by weird creatures and strange ceremonies, and return to a newly transformed and embodied world. On the quest we have encountered red, shaggy monsters who are curiously human (they like to help women and are quick to avenge their honor), and humans slightly monstrous like the lady who ravages bodies and claims heads. We have charted the natural world in sexual terms and embodied the sexual world with natural metaphors. We have accomplished what Lucien Lévy-Bruhl calls in primitive culture "participation mystique,"[72] the interanimation of man and nature, what Léopold Sédar Senghor calls "dancing the Other."[73]

If the riddle solver is a quester thrust into the moment of metaphor, the hero is a solver whose riddle spins out before him in narrative time. He must leave home, confront the dream world of unreal shapes, recognize and be reconciled with the uncanny or kill it, and come home a conqueror or

71. Frye, *Spiritus Mundi*, p. 147.

72. See, for example Lévy-Bruhl's *How Natives Think*, tr. Lilian A. Clare (London: Allen and Unwen, 1926) and *The "Soul" of the Primitive*, tr. Lilian A. Clare (New York: Praeger, 1966). The relationship between the inner world of man and the outer world of nature has always been a prime concern of anthropologists. For Lévy-Bruhl the relationship is precausal and empathetic; for later anthropologists like Claude Lévi-Strauss, it involves the manipulation of natural symbols to fashion a social mirror. But even in Lévi-Strauss, there is a sense of natural myth as an act of empathetic poetry: the "savage mind" ("la pensée sauvage") is also "the wild pansy." This charting of the human abstract with concrete, natural symbols (what Lévi-Strauss calls the "science of the concrete") is of course a fundamental tenet of all imagistic poetry. It is what T. S. Eliot calls the "objective correlative." And the modern poet's view of "participation" is best put by Yeats in a letter to Dorothy Wellesley: "We are happy when for everything inside us there is a corresponding something outside us" (cited by Richard Wilbur, *Responses* [New York: Harcourt, Brace Jovanovich, 1976], p. 103).

73. Léopold Sédar Senghor, *Liberté I: Négritude et Humanism* (Paris: Éditions du Seuil, 1964), p. 259.

seed-king of worlds. Like an unknown riddlic creature, Grendel himself crosses categories, and the hero Beowulf must struggle to discover his meaning. As Nigel Barley shrewdly points out:

> The occurrence of such monster images [in riddles] is of great interest in view of the Anglo-Saxons' concern with such anomalous creatures. The monster Grendel in *Beowulf* is little more than a totally individuated riddle image. Throughout, he is described in terms of an Anglo-Saxon warrior. He has been exiled with all his kin because his ancestor Cain murdered Abel. He refuses to pay compensation to the dwellers of Heorot. He has a hall. He fights the champion of the Danes. On the other hand, he cannot use weapons, his armour is in the form of scales growing on his body and his hall stands at the bottom of a lake in the wastelands. He is the embodiment of all categorical contradictions—a riddle without an answer. Small wonder then that nineteenth century critics treated the poem as a riddle to be solved and were outraged to find that many solutions fitted.[74]

Apart from the nightmare, can we say what Grendel represents in the daylight world of the hall? Perhaps not—as Karsten Harries says of metaphoric shapes: "What metaphor names may transcend human understanding so that our language cannot capture it."[75] Perhaps Grendel's name means that something is grinding in the halls and hearts of men. Beowulf seems implicitly to recognize this when he promises protection to the sons of Hrothgar and when his report to Hygelac suddenly turns from monsters to the monstrous passions of the Heathobard (and by analogy the Danish) court. Somehow the failed peace-weaving of *Beowulf* lends power to the monstrous dream. And Beowulf's slaying of the hall-stalkers merely destroys the vehicle and liberates the tenor of feud-hall passion. Beowulf's battles are no playful, riddlic encounters. The uncanny here has deadly power. There is no conscious raising of the myth, no metaphysical play, no delight in the Other, except as a worthy antagonist. But Grendel as a crosser of categories, a surreal shape, remains a riddle. He is the clawed warrior, the

74. Nigel F. Barley, "Structural Aspects of the Anglo-Saxon Riddle," *Semiotica* 10 (1974): 157.

75. Harries, "Metaphor and Transcendence," *Critical Inquiry* 5 (1978): 74.

flesh-eater, the uninvited hall-thane. He is music- and man-hater, son without father, the unraveler of peace. Speechless he seems to hiss in the dark as he stalks the hall, "Say what I mean."

RIDDLE AND ROOD

The uncanny may sustain as well as destroy. If we riddle the darkness with unknown shapes, we shape recognition in a sacred riddle. Who existed before his mother was born, walked on water, turned water into wine, was married to all and married to none—who rode on the rood, swordless to slay death? The greatest riddle is sung in flesh. Who plays not, perishes. The first and finest dream-revelation of the cosmic riddle to emerge from Western Europe is the Old English lyric, "The Dream of the Rood." The heart of the poem is a recollection in two frames. The dreamer recounts his midnight vision of the rood sometimes clothed in the light of victory, sometimes stained with a terrible blood. As the dreamer struggles like a narrative riddler to say what the mysterious creature means, the rood rises out of the dream like a personified riddle-creature to recall its passionate history as the Christ-tree:

> It was long ago—I remember I was ripped
> From the forest's edge, torn from my trunk,
> Seized by fierce enemies, sheared and shaped,
> Forced to raise hard criminals high—
> A dumb show. Swung onto the shoulders
> Of cruel men, speared into a hill,
> I saw Christ climb like a warrior,
> Coming with a king's zeal. The earth shook:
> I dared not bend or bow down, killing
> Against the Lord's command. I could have crushed
> The fierce men—yet I stood fast.
> The warrior that was God Almighty stripped
> For battle, body-strong and spirit-keen.
> He climbed high on the hated swing—
> Proud in the eyes of many, mounted the gallows
> To save men. I trembled in Christ's clutch:

Unbowed I bore the body of God.
A rood I was raised—I raised the mighty King,
Heaven's Lord, and bent not to earth.
Through my body men drove dark nails,
Blood-iron with a battle-ring: the fierce wounds
Still flow, but my Lord brooked no vengeance.
They mocked us together—I was stained with blood
Borne from the side of God as he sent forth,
His body streaming, a quick spirit.[76]

In its formal structure the poem is a combination of two modes of riddling—in part the dreamer recounts what he saw, in part the creature reveals what it is. In its use of metaphoric disguise and paradox, the poem raises riddle language to the level of sacred mystery. The rood crosses categories: it is tree, artifact, suffering servant, and divine mediator. In this it imitates Christ (as it later exhorts the dreamer to do). In the crucifixion it is paradoxically both servant and slayer—this is the heart of its suffering. As gallows it is a symbol of unholy vengeance; as rood, a token of redemptive love. Christ himself is a riddle incarnate. Like a great warrior (the metaphoric link), he is "battle-strong" and "spirit-keen" (the ground) in service to his lord. Paradoxically he strips instead of arming for battle and embraces his slayer in a self-willed sacrifice that kills death (the gap). The metaphor invites us to be one with Christ; the gap requires us to redefine our traditional notions of heroic action.

Why should the rood imitate Christ and make of the crucifixion a riddle? To allow the warrior to climb to victory? To mediate the awesome and unknown consciousness of a suffering human god? To bring the natural world into the sacred conflict? To convey through the miracle of a talking tree something of the mystery lost in living with the idea of the incarnation? To raise the idea of empathetic play (one in another pretending *I am*) from riddle to redemption? To create in the mystery a metaphor of heaven? However we read the roots of the dream, as the rood exhorts the dreamer "to reveal this vision in words to men," we are reminded in poetic, religious terms of a primitive truth: Who would know (and be initiated into) the mysteries of the tribe must engage in the play of sacred riddles.

76. "The Dream of the Rood," ll. 28–49, *ASPR* 2: 61–62.

Gary Snyder argues in his essay "Poetry and the Primitive," in *Earth House Hold,* that poets, like primitive men, live in a "mythological present in close relation to nature,"[77] that they *inspire* the world (breathing in the song of grass, wind, crow—breathing out the seed-syllables of power), that they sing in concrete images the vibrant connection, what Snyder calls after Whitman "the inner song of the self, and of the planet."[78] The poet's function remains that of the paleolithic shaman—he is a shaper whose "mind reaches easily out into all manners of shapes and other lives, and gives song to dreams."[79] In the dream world of concrete imagery, the poet moves metaphorically toward the Other. Like the Old English riddler, he sings nightingale, fox, fish, bow (once tree), and in singing "makes love to the animals."[80] Primitive peoples, as Claude Lévi-Strauss has shown, weave a world order out of natural myth.[81] The wildcat's relation to the deer or crow may be the metaphoric embodiment of the relationship between tribes or individuals. But the stories of cat and crow are also celebrations of man's meeting the Other. Snyder says:

> People of primitive cultures appreciate animals as other people off on various trips. Snakes move without limbs, and are like free penises. Birds fly, sing, and dance; they gather food for their babies; they disappear for months and then come back. Fish can breathe water and are brilliant colors. Mammals are like us, they fuck and give birth to babies while panting and purring; their young suck their mothers' breasts; they know terror and delight, they play.[82]

Fish breathe water. Birds brood. Snakes move like a phallic mirror. The otter slips into his watery playground. Nature sings with a man-shaped voice. The African poet Senghor calls this celebration *recognition*—being born with the Other:

77. Gary Snyder, *Earth House Hold* (New York: New Directions, 1969), p. 117.
78. Ibid., p. 123.
79. Ibid., p. 122.
80. Ibid., p. 119.
81. See especially *Totemism* and *The Savage Mind.*
82. Snyder, *Earth House Hold,* p. 121.

Man lives symbiotically with the Other; he *knows (con-naît)* and is *born with* the Other in Paul Claudel's terms. Subject and object are here dialectically face to face in the same act of recognition which is the act of love. "I think, therefore I am," wrote Descartes. The observation has already been made: one always thinks some *thing*. The black African might say, "I feel the Other, I dance the Other, therefore I am." For to dance is to create, especially when the dance is a dance of love. . . .

This is an *existentialism* rooted in Mother-Earth, blooming in the sun of Faith. This world-presence is the *participation of the subject with the object*, the participation of man with the cosmic forces, the *communion* of man with other men, and finally, with all *beings* from the smallest stone to God.[83]

This is similar to Richard Wilbur's notion that the poet is like a rain-dancer "trying to establish a *relation* to the rain."[84] The dance cannot literally create the rain—"it is not a mere imitation, but a magic borrowing of the powers it wants to approach, and a translation of what is borrowed into the language of the dancing human body."[85] Inspiration is the breath of song. We breathe in the mysterious green—sunlight dancing on the skin of tree or the belly of grass—and breathe out in images the blood-song of oak or the crushed whisper of noon grass. In charging the universe with human shapes, we escape the bone-house to rage with the storm, mother with the fox, clutch light with the moon, court death with the shield, and rise up with the onion or the Gospel skin. Poetry is play, says Johan Huizinga, and never far from its riddlic roots.[86] "Say what I mean"—"Say who I am." In riddles we shape and celebrate the universe, see and become one with the creatures. We are symbol-makers. We are also, as Snyder says, beautiful animals.[87]

Like the tree, the bird, the moon—we change, but we also chart the changing. We are metamorphic and metaphoric. What we see is in part a function of the way we see. With riddles we celebrate the arms of oak,

83. Senghor, *Liberté I*, pp. 259, 317; the translation first appeared in Senghor's *Selected Poems / Poésies Choisies*, tr. Craig Williamson (London: Rex Collings, 1976), p. 13.
84. Wilbur, *Responses*, p. 219.
85. Ibid.
86. Huizinga, *Homo Ludens*, p. 135.
87. Snyder, *Earth House Hold*, p. 120.

the horns of moon, the wounds of chalice, the belly of bow, the pregnancy of rain. We rediscover what Whitman calls "God in every object"[88] and take delight in dancing the Other. This is not just the pleasure of poetry, but a means of metaphoric learning. In the modern world we must riddle more and ruin less. Our task, as D. H. Lawrence says, is to relate to the living universe:

> If we think about it, we find that our life *consists in* this achieving of a pure relationship between ourselves and the living universe about us. This is how I "save my soul" by accomplishing a pure relationship between me and another person, me and other people, me and a nation, me and a race of men, me and the animals, me and the trees or flowers, me and the earth, me and the skies and sun and stars, me and the moon: an infinity of pure relations, big and little, like the stars of the sky: that makes our eternity, for each one of us, me and the timber I am sawing, the lines of force I follow; me and the dough I knead for bread, me and the very motion with which I write, me and the bit of gold I have got. This, if we knew it, is our life and our eternity: the subtle, perfected relation between me and my whole circumambient universe.[89]

How do we find the right relation to the universe? By meeting the Other on a metaphoric playground, by making riddles, by listening to crow. Two stories from separate cultures, each with its riddlic connection, point the way. Snyder tells of an Arapaho dancer of the Ghost Dance who returns from his trance to sing:

> I circle around, I circle around
>
> The boundaries of the earth,
> The boundaries of the earth
>
> Wearing the long wing feathers as I fly
> Wearing the long wing feathers as I fly.[90]

88. See n. 2.

89. D. H. Lawrence, "Morality and the Novel," in *Phoenix I: The Posthumous Papers* (New York: Viking, 1936), p. 528. The passage quoted was first published under the title "The Universe and Me," by the Powgen Press, New York, in 1935.

90. Snyder, *Earth House Hold*, p. 123.

And Eido Roshi at a recent talk[91] told a story about a Zen master who was walking along a country road with his pupil:

> Suddenly they came upon a goose. The master stretched out his neck and watched intently—and so, watching the master, did the student. The goose suddenly rose, wheeled, and was gone. The master smiled, the student pondered. Suddenly the master turned and asked the student, "Where is the goose?"
>
> Puzzled, the student replied, "The goose is gone, Master." The master grabbed the student's nose and gave it a vicious twist. "Onk," cried out the student in pain.
>
> "Exactly," said the master and walked on down the road.

How do we meet the Other? Wear feathers, tell riddles, imitate the goose. Honk and fly. Honk and fly.

TEXT AND TRANSLATIONS

The translations in this book are based on the texts of the most recent riddle edition, my own, *The Old English Riddles of the Exeter Book* (Chapel Hill: University of North Carolina Press, 1977). Lost portions of the text are indicated by asterisks: some of these are the result of manuscript aging or mutilation; some are indicated by a gap in the meaning or meter of the text and are probably the result of scribal error. I have tried occasionally to fill in the sense of a lost word and have sometimes gathered together bits of words in order to give a glimpse of meaning to fragmentary passages and to avoid an ungainly succession of isolated words and long lacunae. Readers interested in the exact placement of fragments, lost letters, and lacunae should consult the original Old English edition where the system of elliptical indication is more complicated.

Old English poetry is built on an alliterative, strong-stress pattern. Each line contains four strongly stressed syllables—for example:

91. Eido Shimano Roshi, "Meditation Workshop," for Professor Donald K. Swearer's course in "Myth, Symbol, and Ritual in Asian Religions," under the sponsorship of the Margaret Gest Center for the Cross-Cultural Study of Religion, at Haverford College, 11 February 1980. The story is recounted here as best I remember Eido Roshi's telling of it.

1	2	3	4
Ic swiftne	geseah	on swaþe	feran
I a swift (thing)	saw	on the road	travelling

The possible alliterative patterns are 2 and 3, 1 and 3, or 1 2 and 3 (as in the example above). The third stress regularly alliterates, the fourth stress rarely. Often there is cross-line alliteration, sometimes assonance, rarely rhyme. The positioning of unstressed syllables is fairly, though not entirely, free. The Old English poetic lexicon was stocked with a wide variety of words for the important commonplaces of the culture—*hero, battle, sea, horse, hall, death* and so on—which meant that the alliterative demands of a particular line could be readily met. But the mead-hall poet's delight is the modern translator's bane—since cultures rarely show linguistic diversity in the same set of terms (the Eskimo needs many words for snow, the Ngoni warrior needs none). Another difficulty is that what was common to the literate Anglo-Saxon, the controlled strong-stress line, often proves strange to modern readers of poetry used to the iambic rhythms of post-medieval poets or the free verse of many modern writers. Occasional modern poets hearken back to the ancient Anglo-Saxon rhythms—W. H. Auden in *The Age of Anxiety,* [92] Richard Wilbur in "Junk,"[93] and Gerard Manley Hopkins in some lines written in sprung rhythm[94]—but mainly the rhythms remain a medievalist's delight. Translators deal with these problems in different ways. Some attempt to keep to the strict Old English meter and dredge up archaic words to meet the alliterative demands. Some scuttle strong stress for the more comfortable iambic pentameter or free verse. Some struggle to make compromises. My own compromise represents a cross between the traditional Anglo-Saxon meter and a looser form used by Aelfric, sometimes called rhythmical prose.[95] It retains the four-stress line in a loosely alliterative pattern. It builds in abundant cross-line

92. W. H. Auden, *The Age of Anxiety* (New York: Random House, 1947).

93. Richard Wilbur, *The Poems of Richard Wilbur* (New York: Harcourt, Brace Jovanovich, 1963), pp. 9–11.

94. For a description of sprung rhythm, see Harold Whitehall's "Sprung Rhythm," in *Gerard Manley Hopkins,* by Robert Lowell et al. (New York: New Directions, 1945), pp. 28–54.

95. For a description of Aelfric's style, see John C. Pope, ed., *Homilies of Aelfric,* vol. 1 (London: Early English Text Society, 1967), pp. 105–36.

alliteration—especially to bind to the rest of the poem an occasional nonal-literative line. It plays with the possibility of assonance and adds the close repetition of words and morphemes. Occasionally it makes use of perfect or partial rhyme. Take, for example, the *bookworm* riddle (45)—which I quote here in Old English, in a straightforward translation (with some indication of the ambiguities in the original), and in my own poetic render-ing:

> Moðð word fræt—   me þæt þuhte
> wrætlicu wyrd þa ic þæt wundor gefrægn,
> þæt se wyrm forswealg wera gied sumes,
> þeof in þystro, þrymfæstne cwide
> ond þæs strangan staþol. Stælgiest ne wæs
> wihte þy gleawra þe he þam wordum swealg.[96]

A moth ate (spoken) words—to me that seemed
A strange event (weird fate, odd saying), when I heard of that wonder,
That a worm (bug, snake, dragon) should swallow (mentally im-bibe) the songs of a man,
A thief in darkness (ignorance), his glory-fast sayings (munchings),
And their place (intellectual foundation) of strength. That thief-guest
Was no wiser for having swallowed (mentally imbibed) words.

> A moth ate songs—wolfed words!
> That seemed a weird dish—that a worm
> Should swallow, dumb thief in the dark,
> The songs of a man, his chants of glory,
> Their place of strength. That thief-guest
> Was no wiser for having swallowed words.

My poetic translation is written in strong stress meter. It contains two primary alliterative stresses each in lines 1, 2, 3, and 6. The stresses of line 4 are linked by the assonance of "man" and "chants"; of line 5 by the

96. Williamson, *The Old English Riddles of the Exeter Book*, p. 97.

A Feast of Creatures

48

assonance of "strength" and "guest" (or "place" and "strength," depending on the individual pronunciation). Lines 4 and 5 are also linked by the cross-line alliteration in "guest" and "glory." All six lines have an *s* alliterative stress; three lines have a double *w* stress. The sinuous *s* pattern I hope produces some of the ominous overtones of the *wyrm* complex (worm-snake-dragon) in Old English. Verbal repetitions include "songs" (1 and 4), "words" (1 and 6), "swallow"/"swallowed" (2 and 6), and the double "that" of line 2 and triple "of" of lines 4–5. All of these devices help to tighten the translation and in some sense compensate for the loosening which takes place with the loss of primary alliteration in lines 4–5. The translation is occasionally iambic as in "A moth ate songs," or "Their place of strength"; but this momentary pattern is almost always followed by the shock of dense stress, as in "wolfed words," and "thief-guest." I hope this produces a rhythm that rolls back and forth between an ancient and modern mode—it is a rhythm that is influenced by Hopkins's sprung rhythm.

Building into the translation what Fred C. Robinson calls the "artful ambiguities"[97] of the Old English riddle proves a difficult task. The word-gobbling *wyrm* that steals man's cultural songs from their vellum foundation may mean "bug, worm, snake, reptile, or dragon" in Old English. The dragon that destroys Beowulf is a *wyrm*, but so is the larva that spins silk. Building the bug into a dragon and bringing him down is part of the mock-epic game of the riddle,[98] but most of this is lost in the innocuous "worm" of modern English. Taking the ravenous possibilities of *fræt*, a word that seems to imply unnatural gobbling, I try to recapture the dragon's ferocity with the phrase, "wolfed words." *Wyrd* is a word whose meaning ranges from "terrible fate" (epic dragons) to "what's happening" (mocking the bug); in the riddlic context it is also a pun on *gewyrd*, "speech." The ambivalent tone is echoed by *cwide*, "songs, sayings," a pun on *cwidu*, "what is munched."[99] The grotesque irony of this is perhaps conveyed in

97. Fred C. Robinson, "Artful Ambiguities in the Old English 'Book-Moth' Riddle," in *Anglo-Saxon Poetry: Essays in Appreciation: For John C. McGalliard*, ed. Lewis E. Nicholson and Dolores Warwick Frese (Notre Dame, Ind.: University of Notre Dame Press, 1975), pp. 355–62. Much of my discussion in this paragraph derives from Robinson.
98. For the various parodic devices in the riddle, see Ann Harleman Stewart, "Old English Riddle 47 as Stylistic Parody," *Papers on Language and Literature* 11 (1975): 227–41.
99. The puns were first recognized by Robinson.

the "weird dish," since for moderns not only a hard fate but also hot lasagne may be "dished out." The addition of "dumb" is also an attempt to catch the bovine level of *cwidu* as well as the unspeaking idiocy of the worm. The word *þystru* means either physical or mental "darkness"; *swealg*, "swallow physically" or "imbibe mentally." These ambiguities are kept in modern English (e.g., "That book left me in the dark." "Don't swallow that old line."). These are just some of the semantic problems any translator must deal with.

Some readers may object to the trade of a wolf for a dragon or the intrusion of a dish—but a translator must attempt to reproduce not only primary meanings, but also ambiguities, textures, and tones. A safe translation is often one that does injustice to the complexity of the original. My goal has been to recreate faithfully the Old English and to shape modern English poems as compelling as the originals. Just as the riddlic game is a mediation between setter and solver, so too the act of translation is a mediation, a dance of two minds. The Anglo-Saxons themselves, often members of a multilingual community, recognized the complexity of translation. King Alfred describes the act metaphorically in the preface to his translations of Augustine's *Soliloquies:*

> So I gathered staves and posts and tie-beams for each of the tools
> I should work with, and building-timbers and beams for each of the
> structures I should make—as much beautiful wood as I could carry.
> Each time I shouldered the wood home I wanted the forest, but
> it was more than I could carry. In each beam I saw something I
> needed at home. So I urge those who have knowledge and good
> wagons to go to the woods where I cut my beams and fetch their
> own beautiful branches so they can weave lovely walls and shape
> splendid buildings and bright towns and live there joyfully summer
> and winter as I have not yet been able to do.[100]

Each translator rebuilds the Anglo-Saxon world in his own way. For those interested in the comparative variety of shapes, I include in the next section a collection of *bookworm* riddle translations. Some are pedantic, some are

100. Thomas A. Carnicelli, ed., *King Alfred's Version of St. Augustine's Soliloquies* (Cambridge: Harvard University Press, 1969), p. 47 (translation mine).

lively, some are provocative, some sing. Some seem to have been gobbled by a sharp-toothed bookworm and regurgitated. But all of us, scholars and poets, must plead *mea culpa* in trying to translate. Hauling words and ideas from one culture to another is no easy task.

COMPARATIVE TRANSLATIONS: THE BOOKWORM RIDDLE

A moth ate a word. To me it seemed
A marvelous thing when I learned the wonder
That a worm had swallowed, in darkness stolen,
The song of a man, his glorious sayings,
A great man's strength; and the thieving guest
Was no whit the wiser for the words it ate.[101]
—Charles W. Kennedy

A worm ate words. I thought that wonderfully
Strange—a miracle—when they told me a crawling
Insect had swallowed noble songs,
A night-time thief had stolen writing
So famous, so weighty. But the bug was foolish
Still, though its belly was full of thought.[102]
—Burton Raffel

A moth ate words. To me it seemed
a remarkable fate, when I learned of the marvel,
that the worm had swallowed the speech of a man,
a thief in the night, a renowned saying
and its place itself. Though he swallowed the word
the thieving stranger was no whit the wiser.[103]
—Paull F. Baum

101. Charles W. Kennedy, tr., *An Anthology of Old English Poetry* (New York: Oxford University Press, 1960), p. 41.

102. Burton Raffel, tr., *Poems From the Old English*, 2d ed. (Lincoln, Neb.: University of Nebraska Press, 1964), p. 93.

103. Baum, *Anglo-Saxon Riddles*, p. 34.

A moth devoured words. When I heard
of that wonder it struck me as a strange event
that a worm should swallow the song of some man,
a thief gorge in the darkness on a great man's
speech of distinction. The thievish stranger
was not a whit the wiser for swallowing words.[104]
　　　　　　　　　　—Kevin Crossley-Holland

I heard of a wonder, of words moth-eaten;
that is a strange thing, I thought, weird
that a man's song be swallowed by a worm,
his binded sentences, his bedside stand-by
rustled in the night—and the robber-guest
not one whit the wiser for the words he had mumbled.[105]
　　　　　　　　　　—Michael Alexander

A moth ate words; a marvellous event
I thought it when I heard about that wonder,
A worm had swallowed some man's lay, a thief
In darkness had consumed the mighty saying
With its foundation firm. The thief was not
One whit the wiser when he ate those words.[106]
　　　　　　　　　　—Richard Hamer

A moth ate songs—wolfed words!
That seemed a weird dish—that a worm
Should swallow, dumb thief in the dark,
The songs of a man, his chants of glory,
Their place of strength. That thief-guest
Was no wiser for having swallowed words.
　　　　　　　　　　—Craig Williamson

104. Crossley-Holland, *The Exeter Riddle Book,* p. 70.
105. Michael Alexander, tr., *The Earliest English Poems,* 2d ed. (New York: Penguin, 1977), p. 100.
106. Richard Hamer, tr., *A Choice of Anglo-Saxon Verse* (London: Faber and Faber, 1970), p. 107.

SELECTED BIBLIOGRAPHY

For a full bibliography on the Exeter Book riddles and riddle scholarship, see my text edition of 1977 listed below.

RIDDLE EDITIONS

Trautmann, Moritz, ed. *Die altenglischen Rätsel: Die Rätsel des Exeterbuchs.* Heidelberg: C. Winter, 1915.

Tupper, Frederick, Jr., ed. *The Riddles of the Exeter Book.* Boston: Ginn and Co., 1910.

Williamson, Craig, ed. *The Old English Riddles of the Exeter Book.* Chapel Hill: University of North Carolina Press, 1977.

Wyatt, A. J., ed. *Old English Riddles.* Boston: D. C. Heath, 1912.

RIDDLE TRANSLATIONS

Baum, Paull F., tr. *Anglo-Saxon Riddles of the Exeter Book.* Durham, N.C.: Duke University Press, 1963.

Crossley-Holland, Kevin, tr. *The Exeter Riddle Book.* London: Folio Society, 1978. Reissued as *The Exeter Book Riddles.* New York: Penguin, 1979.

Mackie, W. S., ed. and tr. *The Exeter Book,* pt. 2. London: Early English Text Society, 1934.

WORKS ON THE OLD ENGLISH RIDDLES

Adams, John F. "The Anglo-Saxon Riddle as Lyric Mode." *Criticism* 7 (1965): 335–48.

Barley, Nigel F. "Structural Aspects of the Anglo-Saxon Riddle." *Semiotica* 10 (1974): 143–75.

Greenfield, Stanley B. "Lore and Wisdom." In *A Critical History of Old English Literature,* pp. 191–212. New York: New York University Press, 1965.

Hacikyan, Agop. *A Linguistic and Literary Analysis of Old English Riddles.* Montreal: Cassalini, 1966.

Kennedy, Charles W. "The Riddles and Gnomic Verse." In *The Earliest English Poetry,* pp. 131–57. New York: Oxford University Press, 1943.

Nelson, Marie. "The Rhetoric of the Exeter Book Riddles." *Speculum* 49 (1974): 421–40.

Robinson, Fred C. "Artful Ambiguities in the Old English 'Book-Moth' Riddle." In *Anglo-Saxon Poetry: Essays in Appreciation: For John C. McGalliard,* ed. Lewis E. Nicholson and Dolores Warwick Frese, pp. 355–62. Notre Dame, Ind.: Notre Dame University Press, 1975.

Shook, Laurence K. "Riddles Relating to the Anglo-Saxon Scriptorium." In *Essays in Honor of Anton Charles Pegis,* ed. J. Reginald O'Donnell, pp. 215–36. Toronto: Pontifical Institute of Mediaeval Studies, 1974.

Stewart, Ann Harleman. "Kenning and Riddle in Old English." *Papers on Language and Literature* 15 (1979): 115–36.

———. "Old English Riddle 47 as Stylistic Parody." *Papers on Language and Literature* 11 (1975): 227–41.

Tupper, Frederick, Jr. "The Comparative Study of Riddles: Originals and Analogues of the Exeter Book Riddles." *Modern Language Notes* 18 (1903): 97–106.

Walters, Frank. "Language Structure and the Meanings of the Exeter Book Riddles." *Ball State University Forum* 19 (1978): 42–55.

Williams, Edith. "What's So New about the Sexual Revolution? Some

Comments on Anglo-Saxon Attitudes toward Sexuality in Women Based on Four Exeter Book Riddles." *Texas Quarterly* 18 (1975): 46–55.

WORKS ON RIDDLES IN GENERAL

Abrahams, Roger D. "The Literary Study of the Riddle." *Texas Studies in Language and Literature* 14 (1972): 177–97.

Abrahams, Roger D. and Alan Dundes. "Riddles." In *Folklore and Folklife: An Introduction,* ed. Richard M. Dorson, pp. 129–43. Chicago: University of Chicago Press, 1972.

Callois, Roger. "Riddles and Images," tr. Jeffrey Mehlman. *Yale French Studies* 41 (1968): 148–58.

Frye, Northrop. "Charms and Riddles." In *Spiritus Mundi*, pp. 123–47. Bloomington, Ind: Indiana University Press, 1976.

Georges, Robert A. and Alan Dundes. "Toward a Structural Definition of the Riddle." *Journal of American Folklore* 76 (1963): 111–18.

Goldstein, Kenneth S. "Riddling Traditions in Northeastern Scotland." *Journal of American Folklore* 76 (1963): 330–36.

Hamnett, Ian. "Ambiguity, Classification, and Change: The Function of Riddles." *Man* n.s. 2 (1967): 379–91.

Huizinga, Johan. *Homo Ludens: A Study of the Play Element in Culture* (especially chaps. 6 and 7). Boston: Beacon Press, 1955.

Maranda, Elli Köngäs. "The Logic of Riddles." In *Structural Analysis of Oral Tradition*, ed. Pierre Maranda and Elli Köngäs Maranda, pp. 189–234. Philadelphia: University of Pennsylvania Press, 1971.

———. "Theory and Practice of Riddle Analysis." *Journal of American Folklore* 84 (1971): 51–61.

———, ed. *Riddles and Riddling*, a special issue of the *Journal of American Folklore* 89 (1976).

Roberts, John M. and Michael L. Forman. "Riddles: Expressive Models of Interrogation." *Ethnology* 10 (1971): 509–33.

Scott, Charles. "On Defining the Riddle: The Problem of a Structural Unit." *Genre* 2 (1969): 129–42.

———. "Some Approaches to the Study of the Riddle." In *Studies in*

Language, Literature, and Culture of the Middle Ages and Later, ed. E. Bagby Atwood and Archibald Hill, pp. 111–27. Austin, Tex: University of Texas Press, 1969.

Taylor, Archer. *English Riddles from Oral Tradition*. Berkeley and Los Angeles: University of California Press, 1951.

———. *The Literary Riddle before 1600*. Berkeley and Los Angeles: University of California Press, 1948.

———. "The Riddle." *California Folklore Quarterly* 2 (1943): 129–47.

———. "The Varieties of Riddles." In *Philologica: The Malone Anniversary Studies*, ed. Thomas A. Kirby and Henry Bosley Woolf, pp. 1–8. Baltimore, Md.: Johns Hopkins University Press, 1949.

Welsh, Andrew. "Riddle." In *Roots of Lyric*, pp. 25–46. Princeton: Princeton University Press, 1978.

 Part Two

1 ∎

What man is so mind-strong and spirit-shrewd
He can say who drives me in my fierce strength
On fate's road when I rise with vengeance,
Ravage the land, with a thundering voice
Rip folk-homes, plunder the hall-wood: 5
Gray smoke rises over rooftops—on earth
The rattle and death-shriek of men. I shake
The forest, blooms and boles, rip trees,
Wander, roofed with water, a wide road,
Pressed by mighty powers. On my back I bear   10
The water that once wrapped earth-dwellers,
Flesh and spirit. Say who shrouds me
And what I am called who carry these burdens.
Sometimes I plunge through the press of waves
To men's surprise, stalking the sea-warrior's   15
Fathomed floor. The white waves whip,
Foam-flanks flaring, the ocean rips,
The whale's lake roars, rages—
Savage waves beat on the shore, cast rock,
Sand, seaweed, water on the high cliffs   20
As I thrash with the wave-power on my back
And shake under blue, broad plains below.
I cannot flee from the helm of water
Till my lord lifts me to a higher road.
Say, wise man, who it is who draws me   25
From sea-clutch and cover as the deep
Stream stills and white waves sleep.
Sometimes my lord seizes and shoves me,
Muscles me under the broad breast of ground,
Packs my power in a dark, narrow prison,   30
Where the hard earth rides my back.
I cannot flee from the weight of torture,
Yet I shake the home-stones of men:
Horn-gabled mead-halls tremble,

The Riddles

59

Walls quake, perch over hall-thanes,   35
Ceilings, cities shake. The air is quiet
Above the land, the sea broods, silent
Till I break out, ride at my ruler's call—
My lord who laid bonds on me in the beginning,
Creation's chains, so I might not escape   40
His power unbowed—my guardian, my guide.
Sometimes I swoop down, whipping up waves,
Rousing white water, driving to shore
The flint-gray flood, its foam-flanks flaring
Against the cliff wall. Dark swells loom   45
In the deep—hills on hills of dark water,
Driven by the sea, surge to a meeting of cliffs
On the coast road. There is the keel's cry,
The sea-guests' moan. Sheer cliffs wait
Sea-charge, wave-clash, war of water,   50
As the high troop crowds the headland.
There the ship finds a fierce struggle
As the sea steals its craft and strength,
Bears quick cargo through bitter time,
The souls of men, while white terror   55
Rides the waves' back. Cruel and killing
On the savage road—who stills us?
Sometimes I rush through the clouds riding
My back, spill the black rain-jugs,
Rippling streams, crack clouds together   60
With a sharp shriek, scattering light-shards.
Sky-breakers surge over shattered men,
Dark thunder rolls with a battle-din,
And the black rain hums from a wet breast,
Waves from the war-cloud's womb.   65
The dark horsemen storm. There is fear
In the cities in the souls of men when dark
Gliding spectres raise light-sharp swords.
Only a dull fool fears no death-stroke;
He dies nonetheless if the true lord   70

Whistles an arrow from the whirlwind
Streaking rain through his heart. Few
Find life in the rain-shriek's dart.
I urge that battle, incite the clash
Of clouds as I rage through riders' tumult   75
Over sky-streams. Then I bow down
At my lord's command, bear my burden
Close to the land, a mighty slave.
Sometimes I storm beneath the land,
Sometimes rage in the cavern of waves,   80
Sometimes whip the waters from above,
Or climb quickening the clash of clouds.
Mighty and swift—say what I'm called
And who rouses and calms my fierce power.

2 ∎

Sometimes busy, bound by rings,
I must eagerly obey my servant,
Break my bed, clamor brightly
That my lord has given me a neck-ring.
Sleep-weary I wait for the grim-hearted   5
Greeting of a man or woman; I answer
Winter-cold. Sometimes a warm limb
Bursts the bound ring, pleasing my dull-
Witted servant and myself. I sing round
The truth if I may in a ringing riddle.   10

3 ■

I am the lone wood in the warp of battle,
Wounded by iron, broken by blade,
Weary of war. Often I see
Battle-rush, rage, fierce fight flaring—
I hold no hope for help to come   5
Before I fall finally with warriors
Or feel the flame. The hard hammer-leavings
Strike me; the bright-edged, battle-sharp
Handiwork of smiths bites in battle.
Always I must await the harder encounter   10
For I could never find in the world any
Of the race of healers who heal hard wounds
With roots and herbs. So I suffer
Sword-slash and death-wound day and night.

4 ■

The culminant lord of victories, Christ,
Created me for battle. Often I burn
Countless living creatures on middle-earth,
Treat them to terror though I touch them not,
When my lord rouses me to wage war.   5
Sometimes I lighten the minds of many,
Sometimes I comfort those I fought fiercely
Before. They feel this high blessing
As they felt that burning, when over the surge
And sorrow, I again grace their going.   10

5 ∎

My gown is silent as I thread the seas,
Haunt old buildings or tread the land.
Sometimes my song-coat and the supple wind
Cradle me high over the homes of men,
And the power of clouds carries me   5
Windward over cities. Then my bright silks
Start to sing, whistle, roar,
Resound and ring, while I
Sail on untouched by earth and sea,
A spirit, ghost and guest, on wing.   10

6 ∎

I am a mimic with many tongues,
Warbling tunes, shifting tones,
Jugging the city with head-song.
Old night-singer, song-shaper,
Pleasure-poet—I keep a clear calling,   5
Wind melody for men. These sit
Bowed in quiet in the curve of song.
Say who I am who sing like a minstrel
Soft clamor of court and mime the world
In harlequin play, boding bright welcome.   10

7 ∎

I was an orphan before I was born—
Cast without breath by both parents
Into a world of brittle death, I found
The comfort of kin in a mother not mine.
She wrapped and robed my subtle skin,   5
Brooding warm in her guardian gown,
Cherished a changeling as if close kin
In a nest of strange siblings. This
Mother-care quickened my spirit, my natural
Fate to feed, fatten, and grow great,   10
Gorged on love. Bating a fledgling
Brood, I cast off mother-kin, lifting
Windward wings for the wide road.

8 ∎

I was locked in a narrow nest,
My beak bound below the water
In a dark dive; the sea surged
Where my wings woke—my body quickened
From the clutch of wave and wandering wood.   5
Born black, streaked white, I rise
From the womb of waves on the wind's back,
Sailing over seals' bath. Who am I?

9 ∎

My dress is silver, shimmering gray,
Spun with a blaze of garnets. I craze
Most men: rash fools I run on a road
Of rage, and cage quiet determined men.
Why they love me—lured from mind,   5
Stripped of strength—remains a riddle.
If they still praise my sinuous power
When they raise high the dearest treasure,
They will find through reckless habit
Dark woe in the dregs of pleasure.   10

10 ∎

Foot-furrowing, I walk and wound—
Living I ravage the raw land;
Lifeless I bind lord and servant.
Sometimes out of my belly I bring
The rush of drink to the fierce-hearted   5
War-man. Sometimes the arch-wild,
Fierce-footed woman treads my back.
Sometimes the dark-haired, drunken slave
Lifts me up near the night fire
With hot hands—turns, teases,   10
Presses, thrusts, warm and wet,
Down dark ways. Say what I am
Who living plunder the down land
And after death serve man.

11 ∎

I saw six creatures scratch the ground,
Their four lively sisters strutting round;
The house of each, pale skin on shell,
A fine, filament robe hung on a wall,
Well-seen. Though each had been stripped   5
Of a gossamer skin, none was nude
Or raw with pain; but quickened, covered,
And brought to grass and grain by God—
They pecked, strutted, and stripped sod.

12 ■

Once I was a plain warrior's weapon—
Now a stripling prince wraps my body
With bright twists of silver and gold.
Sometimes men kiss me, or carry me to battle
Where I call my lord's companions to wage war.   5
Bright with jewels, I am borne by a horse
Over hard plains, sometimes by the sea-stallion
Over storm waves. Sometimes a woman,
Ring-adorned, fills my breast for the table—
Later I lie stripped of sweet treasure,   10
Hard and headless on the long boards.
Clothed in gold, I may grace the wall
Where men sit drinking, a soldier's gem.
Wound with silver, I sometimes ride
A warrior's horse, swallowing soldier's breath,   15
Blasting battle-song. Sometimes I bring
Bold men to wine, sometimes I sing caution
Or rescue thieves' catch or scatter foes
For my lord. Say what I am called.

13 ∎

I am a warrior with a white throat.
My head and sides are tawny. Two ears
Tower above my eyes. My back and cheeks
Are furred. I bear battle-weapons.
My gait is swift. I lope through green   5
Grass on battle-toes. My song is sorrow
If the slaughter-hound scents the narrow
Hall where I lie hidden with a brood
Of children and we wait nestled in the curve
Of love while death snuffs at the door.   10
The dog drags doom—so quick with terror
I seize my children for a secret flight.
If he bellies down, stalking in my chamber,
I cannot choose to fight—that is fools'
Counsel—I must tunnel a quick road   15
Through a steep hill, paw for the light,
Rush mothered babes through the burrow
Safely on secret streets out the hill-hole.
Brood-free I do not fear the hound's rush.
If the death-foe tracks the fierce mother   20
Through side streets, he will find
A narrow road through Grimsgate and a hard
Meeting on hilltop as I turn battle-tooth
And war-claw on the foe I once fled.

14 ■

In battle I rage against wave and wind,
Strive against storm, dive down seeking
A strange homeland, shrouded by the sea.
In the grip of war, I am strong when still;
In battle-rush, rolled and ripped   5
In flight. Conspiring wind and wave
Would steal my treasure, strip my hold,
But I seize glory with a guardian tail
As the clutch of stones stands hard
Against my strength. Can you guess my name?   10

15 ∎

I guard a full flock of old treasures
In a belly bound by wires. Sometimes
I spit forth death-spears by day—
And slay more surely, the fatter my belly.
Sometimes I swallow battle-weapons,   5
Dark-gleaming spears, arrows that ache,
And snakelike points. My belly is great
In its death-bright hoard, dear to proud warriors
Who may remember what I thrust through my mouth.

16 ■

A strange creature, I cannot speak,
Mix words with men, though I have a mouth
And a broad belly

   * * *

I sailed on a ship crowded with kin.

17 ∎

I saw the smooth-prancing E S R O
H, high-powered and head-bright,
Sail on the plain. The proud one
Held on its back a battle-power,
N A M. On the nailed creature came   5
The O R E H. The wide road carried,
Fierce in its flowing, a bold K W
A H. The journey of these was flash
And glint. Let the wise who catch
The drift of this riddle say what I mean.   10

18 ■

I am a strange creature shaped for battle,
Coated in colors, dear to my lord.
Bright thread lurks and swings in my mail,
Cradles the death-gem, gift of a lord
Who grips and guides my body forward   5
Through the wide rush of war. In the clear
Court of day, I bear the glint of gold,
Bright song of smiths. Often I slay
Soul-bearers with thrust and slash.
Sometimes the hall-king decks me in silver   10
Or garnet praise, raises my power
Where men drink mead, reigns my killing
Or cuts me loose, heart-keen, swing-tired,
Through the broad room of war. Sometimes I sing
Through the throat of a friend—the curse   15
Of weapons. No son will seek vengeance
On my slayer when battle-foes ring death.
My tribe will not count children of mine
Unless I lordless leave the guardian
Who gave me rings. My fate is strange: 20
If I follow my lord and wage war,
Sure thrust of a prince's pleasure,
Then I must stroke in brideless play
Without the hope of child-treasure.
I am bound by an ancient craft to lose   25
That joy—so in sheer celibacy I enjoy
The hoard of heroes. Wrapped with wire
Like a bright fool, I frustrate a woman,
Steal her joy, slake desire. She rants,
Rails, curses, claps hands, chants   30
Unholy incantations—bladed words
In a bloodless battle I cannot enjoy

* * *

A Feast of Creatures
78

19 ∎

Head down, nosing—I belly the ground.
Hard snuffle and grub, I bite and furrow—
Drawn by the dark enemy of forests,
Driven by a bent lord who hounds my trail,
Who lifts and lowers me, rams me down,   5
Pushes on plain, and sows seed.
I am a ground-skulker, born of wood,
Bound by wizards, brought on wheel.
My ways are weird: as I walk one flank
Of my trail is gathering green, the other   10
Is bright black. Through my back and belly
A sharp sword thrusts; through my head
A dagger is stuck like a tooth: what I slash
Falls in a curve of slaughter to one side
If my driving lord slaves well.   15

20 ∎

Sixty rode horses down to the shore—
Eleven were prancers, proud and fine,
Four gleaming white. They champed
For the sea-charge but the channel was deep,
The wave-clash cruel, the banks steep,   5
The current strong—so the spear-proud warriors,
Horses and earls, mounted a wagon,
And under its beam rode the bright wain
Over sea-curve to land. No ox drew the wagon,
No strength of slaves, no road-horse hauling.   10
She was no sea-floater or ground-roller
With her weight. She did not drag water,
Fly down from the air or double back,
But bore earls and white horses from steep
Shore to shore—mounts and their men   15
Over deep water and home safe again.

Wob is my name twisted about—
I'm a strange creature shaped for battle.
When I bend and the battle-sting snakes
Through my belly, I am primed to drive off
The death-stroke. When my lord and tormentor   5
Releases my limbs, I am long again,
As laced with slaughter, I spit out
The death-blend I swallowed before.
What whistles from my belly does not easily pass,
And the man who seizes this sudden cup   10
Pays with his life for the long, last drink.
Unwound I will not obey any man;
Bound tight, I serve. Say what I am.

I'm a strange creature with changing cries—
I can bark like a dog, bleat like a goat,
Honk like a goose, shriek like a hawk.
Sometimes I imitate the eagle's cry,
The gray warrior's "keee," sometimes the call   5
Of the kite, sometimes the scream of the gull,
While I sit singing, a saucy mimic.
My name is spelled with P, A, and G—
Also an M, an I, and an E—
Say what these six letters clearly spell.   10

23 ■

I am a wonderful help to women,
The hope of something to come. I harm
No citizen except my slayer.
Rooted I stand on a high bed.
I am shaggy below. Sometimes the beautiful   5
Peasant's daughter, an eager-armed,
Proud woman grabs my body,
Rushes my red skin, holds me hard,
Claims my head. The curly-haired
Woman who catches me fast will feel   10
Our meeting. Her eye will be wet.

24 ∎

A life-thief stole my world-strength,
Ripped off flesh and left me skin,
Dipped me in water and drew me out,
Stretched me bare in the tight sun;
The hard blade, clean steel, cut,   5
Scraped—fingers folded, shaped me.
Now the bird's once wind-stiff joy
Darts often to the horn's dark rim,
Sucks wood-stain, steps back again—
With a quick scratch of power, tracks   10
Black on my body, points trails.
Shield-boards clothe me and stretched hide,
A skin laced with gold. The bright song
Of smiths glistens on me in filigree tones.
Now decorative gold and crimson dye,   15
Cloisoned jewels and a coat of glory
Proclaim the world's protector far and wide—
Let no fool fault these treasured claims.
If the children of men make use of me,
They will be safer and surer of heaven,   20
Bolder in heart, more blessed in mind,
Wiser in soul: they will find friends,
Companions and kinsmen, more loyal and true,
Nobler and better, brought to new faith—
So men shall know grace, honor, glory,   25
Fortune, and the kind clasp of friends.
Say who I am—glorious, useful to men,
Holy and helpful from beginning to end.

25 ■

I am man's treasure, taken from the woods,
Cliff-sides, hill-slopes, valleys, downs;
By day wings bear me in the buzzing air,
Slip me under a sheltering roof—sweet craft.
Soon a man bears me to a tub. Bathed,   5
I am binder and scourge of men, bring down
The young, ravage the old, sap strength.
Soon he discovers who wrestles with me
My fierce body-rush—I roll fools
Flush on the ground. Robbed of strength,   10
Reckless of speech, a man knows no power
Over hands, feet, mind. Who am I who bind
Men on middle-earth, blinding with rage
And such savage blows that dazed
Fools know my dark power by daylight?   15

26 ■

Part of the earth grows lovely and grim
With the hardest and fiercest of bitter-sharp
Treasures—felled, cut, carved,
Bleached, scrubbed, softened, shaped,
Twisted, rubbed, dried, adorned,   5
Bound, and borne off to the doorways of men—
This creature brings in hall-joy, sweet
Music clings to its curves, live song
Lingers in a body where before bloom-wood
Said nothing. After death it sings   10
A clarion joy. Wise listeners
Will know what this creature is called.

27 ■

I saw a wonderful creature carrying
Light plunder between its horns.
Curved lamp of the air, cunningly formed,
It fetched home its booty from the day's raid
And plotted to build in its castle if it could   5
A night-chamber brightly adorned.
Then over the east wall came another creature
Well known to earth-dwellers. Wonderful as well,
It seized back its booty and sent the plunderer home
Like an unwilling wanderer. The wretch went west,   10
Moved morosely and murderously on.
Dust rose to the heavens, dew fell on earth—
Night moved on. Afterwards no one
In the world knew where the wanderer had gone.

28 ∎

I am sun-struck, rapt with flame,
Flush with glory, flirt with the wind—
I am clutched by storm and touched by fire,
Ripe for the road, bloom-wood or blaze.
My path through the hall is from hand to hand   5
As friends raise me, proud men and women
Clutch and kiss me, praise my power
And bow before me. To many I bring
A ripe bliss, a rich blooming.

29 ■

Middle-earth is made lovely in unmatched
Ways rich and rare. Across the hall
I saw a creature singing—nothing wilder
In the haunts of men. Her shape is strange.
Her beak hung down, her hands and feet   5
Slung up like a shouldered bird—she waits
Song-hungry in the hall of earls her hour
Of craft. She cannot feast or fly about,
Drink man's delight (she dreams of skill,
A task, her art), but begins to dance   10
On a road of hands—brash mute plays dumb,
Gathering glory while a beautiful haunting
Song sails through her strange foot—
A gift of sound. How her long dangling
Legs chant is a wonderful riddle.   15
Jeweled, naked, proud of rings—
She sings like a mighty sister,
Guardian of air, bearing bass brothers
Droned on her neck. Let the song-lifter,
Truth-shaper, name this creature.   20

30 ■

Middle-earth is made lovely in unmatched ways
Rich and rare. I saw a strange creature
Riding the road, weird craft and power
From the workshops of men. She came sliding
Up on the shore, shrieking without sight,   5
Eyes, arms, shoulders, hands—
Sailed on one foot over smooth plains—
Treasure and haul. Her mouth in the middle
Of a hoard of ribs, she carries corn-
Gold, grain-treasure, wine-wealth.   10
The feast-floater brings in her belly food
For rich and poor. Let the wise who catch
The drift of this riddle say what I mean.

31 ■

An awesome beauty angled the wave;
The deep-throated creature called to land,
Laughed loud-lingering, struck terror
Home to men. Her blades honed sharp,
She was slow to battle but battle-grim,   5
Savage wound-worker. The slaughterer
Struck ship-walls, carried a curse.
The cunning creature said of herself:
"My mother, who comes from the kind of women
Dearest and best, is my daughter grown   10
Great and pregnant; so is it known to men
On earth that she shall come and stand
Gracefully on the ground in every land."

32 ■

I saw close to the houses of men
A strange creature that feeds cattle.
By tooth-hoard and nose-haul
(A useful slave), it scruffs the ground,
Scratches at plants, dogs walls   5
Or drags fields for plunder—seeks
A crop-catch and carries it home.
Its prey is bent stalk and weak root;
Its gift is firm grain and full flower
On a glittering plain—growing, blooming.   10

33 ■

The earth was my mother—I was raised
From her cold, wet womb. I know in my mind
I was not woven from hair or wool
By skillful hands. I have no winding
Weft or warp, no thread to sing   5
Its rushing song; no whirring shuttle
Slides through me, no weaver's sley
Strikes belly or back. No silkworms spin
With inborn skill their subtle gold
For my sides, yet warriors call me   10
A coat of joy. I do not fear
The quiver's gift, the deadly arrow's flight.
If you are clever and quick with words,
Say what this strange coat is called.

34 ∎

A strange creature ran on a rippling road,
Its cut was wild, its body bowed,
Four feet under belly, eight on its back,
Two wings, twelve eyes, six heads, one track.
It cruised the waves decked out like a bird,   5
But was more—the shape of a horse, man,
Dog, bird, and the face of a woman—
Weird riddle-craft riding the drift of words—
Now sing the solution to what you've heard.

35 ∎

I saw a creature with its belly behind
Huge and swollen, handled by a servant,
A hard, muscled man who struggled so
That the bulge in its belly burst through its eye:
Its passion—gorge and spill through death,   5
Then rise and fill with second breath
To sire a son and father self.

36 ∎

This strange creature, a stripling boy,
Sought sweet pleasure pumping joy.
His nourishing Bess gave him four
White fountains—murmur and roar—
To the boy's delight. A bystander said,   5
"Alive, that boy will break the downs;
Dead, he'll bind and wrap us round."

37 ■

Writings reveal this creature's plain
Presence on middle-earth, marked by man
For many years. Its magic, shaping power
Passes knowing. It seeks the living
One by one, winds an exile's road,   5
Wanders homeless without blame, never there
Another night. It has no hands or feet
To touch the ground, no mouth to speak
With men or mind to know the books
Which claim it is the least of creatures   10
Shaped by nature. It has no soul, no life,
Yet it moves everywhere in the wide world.
It has no blood or bone, yet carries comfort
To the children of men on middle-earth.
It has never reached heaven and cannot reach   15
Hell—but must live long through the word
And will of the king of creation's glory.
It would take too long to tell its fate
Through the world's web: that would be
A wonder of speaking. Each man's way   20
Of catching the creature with words is true.
It has no limbs, yet it lives!
If you can solve a riddle quickly,
Say what this creature is called.

38 ■

Old is the shaper, eternal the lord
Who rules this earth, the power of world-
Pillars, prince and king, the guardian
Of all, one real and reckoning God
Who moves and holds heaven and earth   5
In his circling song. He shaped my power
In the earth's beginning, in the world's
Unwinding song set me always awakening,
Sleepless—suddenly bound to night,
My eyes close down. He powers middle-earth   10
With a mighty word—in his charge I wind
The world's embrace. The quick breath of spirit
Startles me—I am ghost-shy, yet always
Bolder than the wild boar bristling at bay.
My scent is stronger than incense or rose,   15
Blooming beauty or the flower distilled,
More delicate than the lily curled in a field
Of light—wisps, blossoms, man's delight.
I am sweeter than the musk of the fragrant nard,
Sharper than the stench of the black swamp.   20
I bind all turnings under heaven's roof,
Guide and sustain as God first wrought,
Hold shape and form, rule thick and thin.
I am higher than heaven—at the point-king's
Command I watch and wield his world-treasure,   25
The great shaper's riddle. I see and sense
All things under earth, the hell-caves
Of suffering souls. I am much older
Than the universe, than middle-earth might be,
Yet born a child from yesterday's womb,   30
Glorious to men. I am brighter than rings
And bracelets of gold with their delicate threads.
I am fouler than wood-rot or the reeking slime

Of seaweed washed on the shore. I am broader
Than earth, wider than the green, billowing plain.   35
A hand may seize, three fingers wrap round me.
I am harder and colder than the bitter frost,
The sword of morning that falls on the ground.
I am hotter than Vulcan's flickering fire,
Sweeter than bee-bread laced with honey,   40
Galled as wormwood gray in the forest.
I can gorge like an old giant—bloated,
Bellied—or live sustained without food.
I can fly higher than pernex, eagle, or hawk,
Outstrip the zephyr, swiftest of winds—   45
I am slower than swamp-frog, snail, rainworm,
Quicker than the skittering child of dung
We call beetle. I am heavier than gray stone
Or a clump of lead, lighter than the bug
That dry-foots the water, harder than flint   50
That strikes fire from steel, softer than down
That flutters in the wind, broader than the earth,
Wider than the green, billowing plain.
I weave round the world a glittering cloak,
A kind embrace. No creature catches   55
My pace and power—I am highest of unfathomed
Miracles wrought by God who alone restrains
With eternal might my thundering power.
I am stronger and grander than the mighty whale,
Dark watcher, wielder of the ocean floor.   60
I am feebler than the handworm which the sons
Of men dig from the skin with shrewd skill.
My head is not wound with delicate curls
Of light hair—the lord has left my face,
Head, skin—bare. Now light curls, locks   65
Shine, hair blooms, shoulders down—hangs

Like a miracle. I am bigger and fatter
Than the mast-fed pig who gorges on beech-wood,
Grunts, roots, snuffles up joy, so that now
He   70

        *   *   *

39 ■

This mother sustains the myriad creatures
Of middle-earth—the brightest, the best,
The darkest, the dearest—the children of men
May joyfully own or usefully rule
In this wide world. Without her children   5
We would not survive. How she mothers
And who she is remains a riddle. The wise
And worldly ought to know this creature's name.

40 ∎

Two feathered flappers came together,
Panting and pushing in the open air.
The bright-haired girl, flushed and proud,
Grew big in the belly if the work was good.
Now scholars may need these letters to know   5
What I'm talking about: o and c,
n and e, k and h, and another c.
The tumblers twist to the letters' key
As the treasure-door swings open
So that solvers can see in the heart   10
Of the riddle, craft and play. Carousing men
May know the names of the low-down lovers!

41 ∎

A noble guest of great lineage dwells
In the house of man. Grim hunger
Cannot harm him, nor feverish thirst,
Nor age, nor illness. If the servant
Of the guest who rules, serves well   5
On the journey, they will find together
Bliss and well-being, a feast of fate;
If the slave will not as a brother be ruled
By a lord he should fear and follow,
Then both will suffer and sire a family   10
Of sorrows when, springing from the world,
They leave the bright bosom of one kinswoman,
Mother and sister, who nourished them.
Let the man who knows noble words
Say what the guest and servant are called.   15

42 ∎

A small miracle hangs near a man's thigh,
Full under folds. It is stiff, strong,
Bold, brassy, and pierced in front.
When a young lord lifts his tunic
Over his knees, he wants to greet   5
With the hard head of this hanging creature
The hole it has long come to fill.

43 ■

I heard of something rising in a corner,
Swelling and standing up, lifting its cover.
The proud-hearted bride grabbed at that boneless
Wonder with her hands; the prince's daughter
Covered that swelling thing with a swirl of cloth.   5

44 ∎

A man sat down to feast with two wives,
Drank wine with two daughters, supped with two sons.
The daughters were sisters with their own two sons,
Each son a favored, first-born prince.
The father of each prince sat with his son,   5
Also the uncle and nephew of each.
In the room's reach was a family of five!

45 ■

A moth ate songs—wolfed words!
That seemed a weird dish—that a worm
Should swallow, dumb thief in the dark,
The songs of a man, his chants of glory,
Their place of strength. That thief-guest   5
Was no wiser for having swallowed words.

46 ∎

This bright circle spoke to men,
The tongueless treasure without voice—
The ring wrought power in silence saying,
"Save me, Healer of souls!" Let those
Who read the red-gold's silent song-craft
Catch the incantation, solve the song,
And give their souls to God as the ring said.

5

47 ■

Bound in place, deaf and dumb,
Making a meal of gifts that come
From a man's hand, she swallows daily
Sustaining treasures dearer than gold,
Brought by a servant, a dark thane,   5
Sought by kings, queens, princes—
For benefit and pleasure. What race
Of shapers makes such treasure for the dark,
Dumb lady to swallow is beyond my measure.

48

On earth this warrior is strangely born
Of two dumb creatures, drawn gleaming
Into the world, bright and useful to men.
The scourge of warriors, the gift of foes,
It is tended, kept, covered by women—   5
Strong and savage, it serves well,
A gentle slave to firm masters
Who mind its measure and feed it fairly
With a careful hand. To these it brings
Warm blessings; to those who let it run   10
Wild it brings a grim reward.

49 ∎

I saw four weird fellows traveling
Together as one. This creature seemed swift,
Bolder than birds—left black tracks.
It flew through air and dove under waves.
The warrior who winds all four over gold-   5
Plated roads pushed restlessly on.

50 ∎

I saw two hard captives carried,
Prisoners bound together as one
Punishing creature, under the roof
Of a hall. Close to one captive worked
A Welshwoman—the strong dark slave   5
Wielded power over both in their bonds.

51 ■

I saw a tree towering in the forest,
Bright with branches, a blooming wood,
Basking in joy. It was nurtured by water,
Nursed by soil, till strong in years,
Its fate snapped, turned savage—   5
It suffered slash, rip, wound—
Was stripped in misery, chained dumb,
Its body bound, its head wrapped
In iron trim. Now it muscles a road
With head-might for another grim warrior—   10
Together they plunder the hoard in a storm
Of battle. The first warrior swings
Through dense threat, head-strong,
While the second follows, fierce and swift.

52 ■

The young man came over to the corner
Where he knew she stood. He stepped up,
Eager and agile, lifted his tunic
With hard hands, thrust through her girdle
Something stiff, worked on the standing   5
One his will. Both swayed and shook.
The young man hurried, was sometimes useful,
Served well, but always tired
Sooner than she, weary of the work.
Under her girdle began to grow   10
A hero's reward for laying on dough.

53 ∎

In the high hall of heroes where men
Sat drinking, I saw four splendors
Borne across the floor—a jeweled tree,
Fine grain of the forest, a share of silver,
Bright twisted gold, the shape and symbol   5
Of the rood that raised us like a ladder
To the high heavens before Christ stormed
The walls of hell. The wood's lineage
I sing before men—maple and oak,
Burnished holly, hard yew—together they serve   10
And share one name—wolfshead-tree,
The outlaw's perch. This creature welcomes
Its lord's weapon, hall-gift and treasure,
The gold-hilted sword. If you can with courage
Grasp this riddle, say what the wood is called.   15

54 ∎

I saw the shuttling wood wound a strange,
Struggling creature, slash it brightly
With battle-colors. A board struck
And small spears stuck into the creature
While the bound wood wound fast,   5
Cinching its woe. One of the creature's
Feet was fixed, the other furious—
Swinging high and swaying low.
A bright tree stood by, spun with light
Leaves. What was left by the spears was borne   10
To the hall floor where warriors sat drinking.

55 ∎

The wind carries small creatures
Over hill-slopes and headlands: dark-
Coated, black-bodied, bursting with song—
They chirm and clamor like a troop on wing,
Winding their way to wooded cliff-walls,   5
Sometimes to the halls of men—singing a name-song.

56 ∎

Mighty one-foot works in a field,
Moves not far, rides not much,
Sails not through the sun-bright air,
Heaves not up on the hauling ship,
The studded wood—yet it serves its lord.   5
It swings heavy tail, small head,
Long tongue, no tooth—pumping iron,
It pokes in a pit! It sucks no water,
Swallows no food—yet it jaws deep
Water into the air, catch and carry.   10
It boasts no spirit, life-gift of the Lord,
Yet it serves well. In the sweep of its name
Are several letters—E, w, and s are some.

57 ■

I saw heart-strong, mind-sharp men
Gazing in a hall at a golden ring.
Who turned the ring prayed to God
For abiding peace, the hall guests'
Grace. The bright circle of gold   5
Spoke the name of the savior of good
Men to the gathering, proclaimed to the eye
And mind of man the most glorious token,
Spoke though dumb of the suffering king
To all who could see in its bodied wounds   10
The hard carving of Christ. An unfulfilled
Prayer has no power in heaven; the dark
Soul will not find the city of saints,
The throne of power, the camp of God.
Let the man who knows how the wounds   15
Of the strange ring spoke as it passed round
The hall—twisting, turning in the hands
Of proud men—explain the riddle.

58 ∎

Rooted near water, raised by the shore,
I was earth-fast, bound in a bed,
My native land. Few men walked
In this wilderness, watched as the wave
Played round my body with its dark arms   5
At dusk and dawn. I did not dream
That someday I should speak, slip words
Over benches, mouthless in the mead-hall.
That is a miracle to men who do not know
This craft—how the point of a knife,   10
A skilled right hand and a man's intent
Tooling together should shape me so
That boldly I bring you my message,
Singing in silence so no man in the wider
World may share our words and understand.   15

59 ∎

Sometimes a lady, comely and proud,
Locks me up, boxes me tight—
Sometimes draws me out on demand
And hands me over to her pleasing prince
Who shoves his hard head in my hole,   5
Slides up while I slip down—
A tight squeeze. If the man who seizes me
Presses with power, something shaggy
Will fill me up, muscle me out—
A precious jewel. Say what I mean.   10

60 ∎

I am the hard punch and pull of power,
Bold thrusting out, keen coming in,
Serving my lord. I burrow beneath
A belly, tunneling a tight road.
My lord hurries and heaves from behind   5
With a catch of cloth. Sometimes he drags me
Hot from the hole, sometimes shoves me
Down the snug road. The southern thruster
Urges me on. Say who I am.

61 ∎

Gleaming with joy, glad with gold,
I am carried to the hall where I serve
Bold heroes carousing together.
Sometimes in a chamber as I come full-
Bodied to a palate, a man may kiss me,   5
Press me boldly with his cupped hand,
Work his will, drink desire,
Mouth on mine, in a delicate spill
        *   *   *
So the light shows what I bear in my belly
        *   *   *
So the reckless man raises this treasure,   10
Drinks deep of my own dark pleasure.

The Riddles

123

62 ■

H O____ I saw smooth-prancing the plain,
Carrying M A__ . A bold H A__
Was to both on that journey the lifter's joy
And a portion of power. The hard H E__
Rejoiced in the going; the F A_____ flew   5
Over the S__ T R____ of that strange troop.

63 ■

A stalk of the living, I nothing said;
Dumb, stand waiting to join the dead.
I have risen before and will rise again
Though plunderers carve and split my skin,
Bite through my bare body, shear my head,   5
Hold me hard in a slicing bed.
I do not bite a man unless he bites me,
But the number of men who bite is many.

64 ■

I stretch beyond the bounds of middle-earth,
Shrink down smaller than a hand-worm,
Grow brighter than the moon, and run
Swifter than the sun. I cradle oceans,
Lakes, paths, green plains in my arms.   5
I dive down under Hell's way and rise up
Over Heaven's home, arced over angels.
I form-fill all earth and ancient worlds,
Fields and sea-streams. Say who I am.

65 ∎

In the hall of the High King I heard
That a voiceless creature spoke charmed
Words, chanted praise, prayer-song
      *   *   *
Wise and wonderful it seemed to me
      *   *   *
It speaks without mouth, moves without feet   5
      *   *   *
Saying, "I am now teacher of men,
Preacher to many on middle-earth—
I will live as long as men walk the land."
Wound with silver and plated gold,
I have seen it open where men sit   10
Drinking together. Now a wise man
Should know what this creature is called.

66 ■

I saw a creature wandering the way:
She was devastating—beautifully adorned.
On the wave a miracle: water turned to bone.

67 ∎

She shapes for her listeners a haunting sound
Who sings through her sides. Her neck is round
And delicately shaped; on her shoulders draped,
Beautiful jewels. Her fate is strange

        *   *   *

68 ■

Who am I who stand so boldly by the sea-road—
High-towering, cheek-bright, useful to men?

69 ∎

Power and treasure for a prince to hold,
Hard and steep-cheeked, wrapped in red
Gold and garnet, ripped from a plain
Of bright flowers, wrought—a remnant
Of fire and file, bound in stark beauty   5
With delicate wire, my grip makes
Warriors weep, my sting threatens
The hand that grasps gold. Studded
With a ring, I ravage heir and heirloom
      *   *   *
To my lord and foes always lovely   10
And deadly, altering face and form.

70 ■

          *   *   *

Often I tugged at four sweet brothers,
Pumped and plied for a day's full drink
At each dangling hole—but the dark herdsman
Pulled my pleasure as I grew older,
And I was drawn to wider roads—moors,   5
Fields—bound by beam and neck-ring
To earth-trace and a gait of suffering,
Haul of sorrow. I kept silence,
Goaded by iron, side-sting—
Moaned to no man, even as punishing   10
Point and pace together tracked pain.

I grew in the ground, nourished by earth
And cloud—until grim enemies came
To take me, rip my living from the land,
Strip my years—shear, split, shape me
So that I ride homeless in a slayer's hand,   5
Bent to his will. A busy sting,
I serve my lord if strength and strife
On the field endure and his hold is good.
We gather glory together in the troop,
Striker and death-step, lord and dark lunge   10
*   *   *
My neck is slim, my sides are dun,
My head is bright when the battle-sun
Glints and my grim loving lord bears me
Bound for war. Bold soldiers know
That I break in like a brash marauder,   15
Burst the brain-house, plunder halls
Held whole before. From the bone-house
One breaks ready for the road home.
Now the warrior who feels the thrust
Of my meaning should say what I'm called.   20

72 ∎

I was a gray girl, ash-haired, elegant,
And a singular warrior at the same time.
I flew with birds and swam in the sea,
Dove under waves, dead among fish,
And stood on the shore—locking in a living spirit.   5

73 ∎

I saw a swift one shoot out on the road:
S S I P.
I saw a woman sitting alone.

74 ■

Suckled by the sea, sheltered near shore,
Cradled in the cold catch of waves,
Footless and fixed—often I offered
To the sea-stream a stretch of mouth.
Now a man will strip my bonelike skin   5
From the sides of my body with a bright blade
And bolt my flesh, relish me raw:
A quick cuisine—crack to jaw.

75 ∎

Often on floodways, found with kin
   * * *
I took for my food
   * * *
       and also him.
Never sat at home
   * * *
Killed in the sea with strange skill   5
And savage power, covered by waves.

76 ■

I am a prince's property and joy,
Sometimes his shoulder-companion,
Close comrade in arms, king's servant,
Lord's treasure. Sometimes my lady,
A bright-haired beauty, lays serving   5
Hands on my body, though she is noble
And the daughter of an earl. I bear
In my belly what blooms in the wood,
The bee's delight. Sometimes I ride
A proud horse in the rush of battle—   10
Harsh is my voice, hard is my tongue.
I bear the scop's meed when his song is done.
My gift is good, my way winning,
My color dark. Say what I'm called.

77 ■

I am puff-breasted, proud-crested,
Swollen-necked. I strut on one foot.
I sport a fine head, high tail,
Eyes, ears, back, beak, two sides.
I ride a stiff nail, my perch above men.   5
I twist in torment when the forest-shaker
Whips and shoves; where I stand the storm-
Wind-waters roll, hail stones,
Sleet shrouds, frost slips freezing,
Snow drifts down. One-foot, hole-belly,   10
I mark the seasons with a twist of fate
I cannot change. My stake is grim.

78 ■

When this creature comes, it gobbles ground,
Grubs earth, follows on its feet
      *   *   *
With no skin or flesh, it always
      *   *   *

79 ∎

My race is old, my seasons many,
My sorrows deep. I have dwelt in cities
Since the fire-guardian wrought with flame
My clean beginning in the world of men,
Purged my body with a circling fire.   5
Now a fierce earth-brother stands guard,
The first to shape my sorrow—I remember
Who ripped our race, hard from its homeland,
Stripped us from the ground. I cannot bind
Or blast him, yet I cause the clench of slavery   10
Round the world. Though my wounds are many
On middle-earth, my strength is great.
My craft and course, power and rich passage,
I must hide from men. Say who I am.

80 ∎

This mother of many well-known creatures
Is strangely born. Savage and fierce,
She roars and sings, courses and flows,
Follows the ground. A beautiful mover,
Prone to power—her clutch is deep.   5
No one knows how to catch her shape
And power in song, or how to mark
The strength of her kin in myriad forms:
Her lineage sings the spawn of creation.
The high father broods over one flow,   10
Beginning and end, and so does his son,
Born of glory, and the heavenly spirit,
The ghost of God. His precious skill

                    *   *   *

All kinds of creatures who lived on the earth
When the garden was graced with beauty and joy.   15
Their mother is always mighty and pregnant,
Sustained in glory, teeming with power,
Plenty, a feast of being, a natural hoard
For rich and poor. Her power increases
Her manifest song. Her body is a burbling   20
Jewel of use, a celibate gem with a quick,
Cleansing power—beautiful, bountiful,
Noble and good. She is boldest, strongest,
Greediest, greatest of all earth-travelers
Spawned under the sky, of creatures seen   25
With the eyes of men. She is the weaver
Of world-children's might. A wise man
May know of many miracles—this one
Is harder than ground, smarter than men,
Older than counsel, more gracious than giving,   30
Dearer than gold. She washes the world
In beautiful tones, teems with children,
Soothes hard suffering, crushes crime.

She wraps the world in a coat of jewels
That amazes man. She is rock-cover,   35
Storm-song, ice-wall, earth's kiss.
She dies without feeling and is born again,
Mother and offspring. Her womb is split

          *   *   *

Open your word-hoard and make known to men
Who the great mother is with her mighty kin.   40

81 ∎

Shunning silence, my house is loud
While I am quiet: we are movement bound
By the Shaper's will. I am swifter,
Sometimes stronger—he is longer lasting,
Harder running. Sometimes I rest   5
While he rolls on. He is the house
That holds me living—alone I die.

82 ∎

A weird creature came to a meeting of men,
Hauled itself in to the high commerce
Of the wise. It lurched with one eye,
Two feet, twelve hundred heads,
A back and belly—two hands, arms,   5
Shoulders—one neck, two sides.
Untwist your mind and say what I mean.

83 ∎

I saw a creature with a strange belly
Huge and swollen, handled by a servant,
Hard-muscled and hand-strong, a mighty man
Who seized the creature, gripped it so
That the tooth of heaven began to blow   5
Out through its eye. It struggled and sang,
Bellowed from below, puffed up and passed out;
Yet it always arched up on air again.

84 ∎

We stood, tall hard twins, my brother
And I—pointed and perched on a homeland
Higher and nobler for our fierce adorning.
Often the forest, dear sheltering wood,
Was our night-cover, rain-shield for creatures   5
Shaped by God. Now grim usurpers
Must steal our homeland glory, hard young
Brothers who press in our place. Parted,
We suffer separate sorrows. In my belly
Is a black wonder—I stand on wood.   10
Untwinned I guard the table's end.
What hoard holds my lost brother in the wide
World I will never know. Once we rode
The high side of battle, hard warriors
Keeping courage together—neither rushed   15
To the fray alone. Now unwhole creatures
Tear at my belly. I cannot flee.
The man who follows my tracks of glory
For wealth and power, in a different light
May find what is wholly for his soul's delight.   20

85 ▪

I saw a creature with a strange belly
Bound in leather
       *   *   *
A servant held it hard from behind,
Sometimes shoved with great skill
       *   *   *
               ate afterwards,   5
Thankful for food at such a time.

86 ▪

I saw a strange sight: a wolf held tight by a lamb—
The lamb lay down and seized the belly of the wolf.
While I stood and stared, I saw a great glory:
Two wolves standing and troubling a third—
They had four feet; they saw with seven eyes!   5

87 ∎

My head is struck by a forging hammer,
Sheared close by a shaping blade,
Honed smooth by a fierce file.
Sometimes I swallow my tempered foe,
When bound by rings, I heave from behind,   5
Thrust a long limb through a hard hole,
Catch hard the keeper of the heart's pleasure,
Twist with my tongue and turn back
The midnight guardian of my lord's treasure
When the conquering warrior comes to hold   10
The gift of slaughter, the joy of gold.

88 ∎

Boast of brown snufflers, tree in the wood,
High hardy life, plant and pleasure,
Earth-shoot, love letter, lady's delight—
Gold-skinned treasure of the high courts—
Ring-bound, the warrior's weapon and joy   5

        *   *   *

89 ∎

I was point and high pleasure for my lord
   * * *
Sometimes startled he broke for the wood,
Sometimes leapt with the years' lean grace
Over plunging streams, sometimes mounted
Steep cliff-trails home or sought hoof-proud   5
In hollows the horned shield of the troop—
Sometimes pawed at ice-grass locked like stone,
Sometimes the gray frost shook from his hair.
I rode my fierce lord's butting brain-chair
Till my younger brother stole helm and headland.   10
Cast homeless to the brown blade, seized
By burnished steel, gutted without gore—
I felt no blood-rush, wept no death-song,
Dreamed no dark vengeance. I endured
The sharp torments of shield-biters.   15
Now I swallow black wood and water,
Bear in my belly dark stain from above.
One-foot, I guard black treasure seized
By a plundering foe that once bore
The battle-companion of the wolf far: 20
The scavenger darts from my belly blackened
And steps toward the table, the stout board
   * * *
Sometimes a share of death when the day-candle
Slides down and no man's eyes see my work
   * * *

90 ∎

I am higher than heaven, brighter than sun,
Harder than steel, smoother than

      *   *   *

            sharper than salt,
Dearer than light, lighter than wind.

91 ∎

I am noble, known to rest in the quiet
Keeping of many men, humble and high born.
The plunderers' joy, hauled far from friends,
Rides richly on me, shines signifying power,
Whether I proclaim the grandeur of halls,   5
The wealth of cities, or the glory of God.
Now wise men love most my strange way
Of offering wisdom to many without voice.
Though the children of earth eagerly seek
To trace my trail, sometimes my tracks are dim.   10

 **Part Three**

NOTES AND COMMENTARY

The Commentary contains a discussion of individual riddles, their probable and possible solutions, their sources and analogues if any, their literary play, and the critical and cultural contexts in which they may usefully be viewed. In sketching both medieval and postmedieval literary treatments of riddle subjects, themes, and techniques, I have tried to indicate how the riddles may be seen as an important and integral part of a continuing literary tradition. Unless otherwise noted, all translations from the Latin and Old English in the Commentary are my own. Most of the original passages from which the translations are taken may be found in the Commentary of my earlier language-text edition of *The Old English Riddles of the Exeter Book* under the appropriate riddle numbers. There the reader will also find a fuller critical apparatus including a history of proposed solutions and variant readings for each riddle. Translations of the medieval Latin riddles are based on the various texts gathered together under the title *Variae Collectiones Aenigmatum Merovingicae Aetatis,* in volumes 133 and 133A of the *Corpus Christianorum, Series Latina,* edited by Fr. Glorie. Translations from Pliny's *Natural History* are based on the Loeb Library texts edited by H. Rackham and W. S. Jones (in making my own translations of Pliny, I have frequently found the editors' suggestions helpful). Translations from *Beowulf* are based on the edition by Fr. Klaeber. Riddle translations in both text and notes are taken from my language-text edition of *The Old English Riddles of the Exeter Book.* All other translations of Old

English poems are based on *The Anglo-Saxon Poetic Records,* edited by George Philip Krapp and Elliott Van Kirk Dobbie. In quoting postmedieval, premodern poetry in the Notes and Commentary, I have exercised the editor's normal prerogative of modernizing spellings and of choosing between alternate punctuations in an attempt to bring the most easily readable texts before an audience of nonspecialists. Normally in making such editorial judgments I have consulted previous readings and renderings before making my own and have followed a tradition of common editorial judgment where possible. Modern poems quoted in the Notes and Commentary remain editorially untouched. Line references are normally given for passages from longer poems, but not for the shorter poems where the passages may easily be found. Citations in this section have been kept brief to keep from piling notes upon notes. Fuller references may be found in the bibliography which concludes the section or in the language-text edition cited above. My aim here has been to create a commentary accessible to the general reader which reflects back upon the text of the riddles like a proper mirror and thus to keep the scholarly glass from turning needlessly and opaquely upon itself.

RIDDLE 1

This creature seems at first glance an odd parcel of storms and natural disasters. It begins with a windstorm wreaking havoc upon the land (lines 1–13), then shifts to a submarine earthquake and resulting sea storm (14–27); a landlocked earthquake follows (28–41), destroying horn-gabled halls and whole cities. Back at sea, the wind drives the flint-gray flood against cliff walls and doomed ships (42–57). A great thunderstorm follows, driving fire-spirits with their light-sharp swords against men (58–78). The several storms are summed up at lines 79–84. To a modern reader this pack of storms may seem a clutch of creatures (and sometimes the riddle is edited into separate *storm* riddles), but the weight of medieval cosmological evidence suggests that the Anglo-Saxons considered all these natural disturbances, from cloudburst to earthquake, part of the dread atmospheric power of the *wind.* In their characterization of the wind as the source of storms and other natural disasters, medieval cosmologists followed a Greco-

Roman, later patristic, tradition stretching from Plato to Bede. Pliny, for example, in book 2 of his *Natural History* (2.38), says that most natural storms the world is heir to come from the sublunar region that he calls the "realm of the winds":

> From the vaporous region below the moon come clouds, thunder-claps, lightning bolts, hail, frost, rain, storms, and whirlwinds—most of mortals' misfortunes and the great wars of nature. . . . Rains fall, clouds rise, rivers dry up, hailstorms sweep down, the sun's rays scorch, gather from earth's corners, drink moisture, and rise again. Steam lowers and rises. Empty winds sweep down, plunder, and roll home. . . . As nature swings back and forth like a sling, discord is kindled by the world's motion. The battle whirls round the world. . . . This is the realm of the winds—here their nature rules.

Likewise earthquakes and submarine tremors are said to arise when wind trapped in earth-caverns and sub-sea-chambers bursts its bonds. This characterization of the battle-storm wind informs much of classical and medieval literature. Two examples may suffice—the first a portion of the Vergilian storm in book 1 of the *Aeneid* (in John Dryden's seventeenth-century translation), the second from a Latin storm poem written by the seventh-century English churchman Aldhelm or a member of his circle (the authorship of the poem, "Lector, casses catholice," is currently the subject of some debate):

> [Aeolus] hurled against the mountain side
> His quivering spear, and all—the god applied.
> The raging winds rush through the hollow wound,
> And dance aloft in air, and skim along the ground;
> Then settling on the sea, the surges sweep,
> Raise liquid mountains, and disclose the deep.
> South, East, and West, with mixed confusion roar,
> And roll the foaming billows to the shore.
> The cables crack, the sailors' fearful cries
> Ascend, and sable night involves the skies;
> And heaven itself is ravished from their eyes.
> Loud peals of thunder from the poles ensue,

Then flashing fires the transient light renew:
The face of things a frightful image bears,
And present death in various forms appears.
                    [Dryden's *Aeneid*, 1.120–34]

   At night the cold winter's
     Storm-wind rises, strikes,
  Savages the land. This air-fury
     Breaks its peace-pact, hurls
  Wine-drunk across heaven: its fist
     Of chaos, earth's bond.

. . . .

  Pale fire flashes across the peaks
     Of heaven—lightning streams down.
  The sky is a gorge of flame.
     Clouds crack and clash.
  The dark wave ravages the strand.
     Whirlwind (vortex and eye,
  Rest and ruin) rides the salt foam.
     The deep rage boils up like winter soup.
  The hurricane sea rides like a wind-warrior
     Storming headlands, shock-waves
  On shock-waves, crashing victory's thunder.
                    [Lines 19–26, 93 ff., *Aldhelmi
                    Opera*, pp. 525 ff.]

The tradition of wind as dread destroyer is continued and refined in later English poetry. In Shelley's "Ode to the West Wind," the poet calls the wild wind's loose clouds "angels of rain and lightning," and says:

           There are spread
    On the blue surface of thine airy surge,
    Like the bright hair uplifted from the head

    Of some fierce Maenad, even from the dim verge
    Of the horizon to the zenith's height,
    The locks of the approaching storm. Thou dirge

Of the dying year, to which this closing night
Will be the dome of a vast sepulchre,
Vaulted with all thy congregated might

Of vapours, from whose solid atmosphere
Black rain, and fire, and hail will burst: O, hear!

In our age, Ted Hughes has also celebrated the warlike power of the windstorm in his poem, "Wind," from *The Hawk in the Rain;* the poem begins:

This house has been far out at sea all night,
The woods crashing through darkness, the booming hills,
Winds stampeding the fields under the window
Floundering black astride and blinding wet

Till day rose; then under an orange sky
The hills had new places, and wind wielded
Blade-light, luminous black and emerald,
Flexing like the lens of a mad eye.

So the Old English "wind" riddle continues a classical tradition and marks
the onset of an English tradition. The riddle characterizes the wind as a
warring creature wreaking havoc upon the land and sea, destroying the high
halls and bone-houses (bodies) of men. The riddler asks not only, "Who
is this destroyer?" but also, "Who shapes and drives the destroyer?" Is this
dark lord an Anglo-Saxon Aeolus, a Nordic sky-father, the Old Testament
God of Wrath, the relentless Wyrd of Germanic myth, an Apocalyptic
Reaper, or the God of Nature in a postlapserian world? Is this fierce
portrayal the riddler's way of raising the Augustinian question about the
nature and origin of evil? And why in a collection which includes such
sustaining creatures as "Creation or Nature" (riddle 38) and "Water"
(riddle 80), should the riddler or the editor of the Exeter Book choose to
open with a natural warrior of such dread power? Perhaps the storm is set
at the beginning of the riddles to remind us of the transience of the world,
as the poet of "The Wanderer" says:

Sea-storms pound cliff-slopes, snowstorms
Bind earth in the white clutch of terror:
The dark shadow slips in from the north,
Slinging hailstones in its feud with men.
Hard and sharp are the days of men
As fate spins the world's web.
Here a man passes—his goods are gone.
Here a woman passes—no friends linger on.
This world-stall will be empty!

There are many possible responses to this truth—despair, grim laughter, the religious quest, a quickened joy in small pleasures. Perhaps the riddler is reminding us as we pass through this gateway to the riddlic world beyond, that to celebrate the beauty and glory of the world's creatures is to realize ourselves as part of the world of metamorphosis—and that means dying as well as living. Wallace Stevens, the great modern poet of metamorphosis, says in "Sunday Morning" that "Death is the mother of Beauty." Perhaps that is the truth the storm-riddler wishes us to know as we pass into the glittering and mysterious world of riddlic creatures.

RIDDLE 2

This is probably the most perplexing riddle in the Exeter collection. Many of its features are still debated by the critics. What is the cold creature that paradoxically obeys its own servant? Is the servant a man or a companion creature? Does the creature "break" or "break into" its bed? Does "sleep-weary" mean "weary with lack of sleep" or "weary with too much sleep"? Why the feud between grim-hearted humans and the winter-cold creature? What is the warm limb that bursts the creature's bound ring? Is it a human limb (finger, arm, leg), a tree limb, the metaphoric limb of the creature itself? All these things are possible, given the ambiguities of the Old English text. Solutions to the riddle have included *millstone, bell, lock, flail,* and *quill pen.* One critic even argues that the poem is a necromancer's tale about a dead man called from the grave to wear the oracular collar. Good arguments can be made for the millstone which breaks its bed of grain (its

warm limb is the friction-heated pivot that breaks its socket) and for the
bell whose clapper breaks its cold bed of silence (the warm limb may be
either the clapper or the bell-ringer's hand)—but many, myself included,
feel the riddle is still unsolved.

RIDDLE 3

This fierce wooden warrior, the *shield*, is the first of many weapon riddles
in the Exeter collection—others include the horn (12, 76), an unknown
creature that swallows and spits battle-treasures (15), the sword (18, 69),
bow (21), coat of mail (33), ram (51), sword box or rack (53), helmet (59),
and spear (71). War and violence were an ever-present part of Anglo-Saxon
life—as is clear in the following grim catalogue of fates in "The Fortunes
of Men":

> Sometimes a fierce fate follows a man—
> A gray wolf may eat him and his mother mourn
> (Man's power is small in the savage world).
> Hunger haunts, the storm slays, the spear guts—
> War is his stalker, battle his bane.
> Blind-eye gropes with his hands through life,
> Lame-foot crawls sinew-sick through pain,
> Bird-man flies wingless from the tree
> Doing wind-tricks (till root-sick his bloom is done).
>
> . . . .
>
> The gallows-rider hangs high, his bone-chest broken,
> His soul-frame done. A dark raven feeds on his eyes.
> No quick hands shield him from the plundering bird.
> His life is lost, his spirit shrouded, his name cursed.
>
> . . . .
>
> The sword slays one at the mead-bench,
> Angry ale-quencher, wine-weary man—
> His words were quick (his life short).

In the Anglo-Saxon world of violence, vengeance, Viking hostility, and
often internecine war, it is no wonder that warriors came well-equipped,
as did Beowulf's band to the dangerous hall of Heorot (321 ff.):

Their war-corselets shone, hard and hand-locked
(The glittering ring-iron groaned in battle)—
Grim guests came to the hall in war-gear.
The sea-weary thanes set their broad shields down—
Hard roofs for battle-rain—by the building's wall,
Came to the mead-benches, mail-coats ringing,
The war-shirts of men. Sea-men stacked
Ash-spears together, steel-gray at the top,
Armed warriors iron-proud of battle-weapons.

Anglo-Saxon shields were made of wood, sometimes covered with leather, and embossed with metal fittings and ornamental mounts. The shield of the riddle is a super-warrior who can withstand greater blows than any man; yet unlike man it has no naturally rejuvenative power, and so it continues to endure blows without the hope of a doctor's healing—a creature hard to kill or to cure. The "hard hammer-leavings" and the "battle-sharp / Handiwork of smiths" are both kennings referring to the shield's enemy, the sword.

RIDDLE 4

This warrior of Christ, benefactor and scourge, comfort and burn, is the *sun.* The association of Christ with the twin-aspect sun probably derives from a prophetic description of the Advent of the Lord in the Book of Malachi (4.1–2):

> For behold, the day comes, burning like an oven, when all the
> arrogant and all evildoers will be stubble; the day that comes shall
> burn them up, says the Lord of hosts, so that it will leave them
> neither root nor branch. But for you who fear my name the sun
> of righteousness shall rise, with healing in its wings.

Church fathers like Isidore of Seville and Gregory the Great commented that Christ would appear on Judgment Day like a great sun whose fiery countenance would warm and comfort the righteous while fiercely tormenting the damned. This tradition is repeated in the Old English poetic *Christ* (899 ff.) in a description of the Advent sunrise:

Then suddenly to Mount Sion out of the southeast
Shall come the blazing light of the Shaper's sun
Brighter than dreams may know—the glittering Son
Of God gliding through the vaults of heaven,
The glorious countenance of Christ the King
Glaring out of eastern skies, fresh to followers,
Fierce to foes, savior and scourge,
Unlike to each—the righteous and wretched.

In Old English the words for son (*sunu*) and sun *(sunne)* are not homo-
phonic, but the similarity of sound suggests the possibility of wordplay. In
later English poetry the association is strengthened by the pun. George
Herbert's seventeenth-century poem "The Son" is a good example of this.
It concludes:

How neatly do we give one only name
To parents' issue and the sun's bright star!
A son is light and fruit; a fruitful flame
Chasing the father's dimness, carried far
From the first man in the East, to fresh and new
Western discoveries of posterity.
So in one word our Lord's humility
We turn upon him in a sense most true:
For what Christ once in humbleness began,
We him in glory call, *The Son of Man.*

RIDDLE 5

The creature that lifts its song-spun coat to the wind is the *whistling* or
whooper swan whose melodious wings are celebrated as early as Homer's
shorter "Hymn to Apollo" and Aristophanes' *The Birds.* In medieval tradition, Gregorius Nazianzenus, a fourth-century Bishop of Constantinople,
tells of a musical competition between some scurrilous swallows and the
strange swans. The whistling swans remain silent while the swallows chatter
with low-class bravado and self-praise; then the swans raise their mysterious
wings to the wind, producing a sweet and winning sound. The phenome-

non of the musical wings is also mentioned in an Old English song of praise
to another bird, "The Phoenix" (131 ff.):

> The sound of [the phoenix's] voice is sweeter and brighter,
> More beautiful than the song-craft of any creature—
> No trumpet or horn or harp's melody
> Can match that sound—no human voice,
> No chanted song, no swan's feathers—
> None of the sounds the Lord has shaped
> For man's joy in the sad-hearted world.

The Old English riddler carries on the conceit of the song-coat in his
haunting lyric. The sense of the bird caught between worlds may owe
something to the patristic notion of the mind or soul as a kind of spiritual
traveler, or to the Nordic belief that questing or liberated souls often take
on birdlike forms. That the strange swans haunt the mind of man is
undeniable—the most brilliant modern evocation of this being the central
verses of Yeats's "The Wild Swans at Coole":

> The nineteenth autumn has come upon me
> Since I first made my count;
> I saw, before I had well finished,
> All suddenly mount
> And scatter wheeling in great broken rings
> Upon their clamorous wings.

> I have looked upon those brilliant creatures,
> And now my heart is sore.
> All's changed since I, hearing at twilight,
> The first time on this shore,
> The bell-beat of their wings above my head,
> Trod with a lighter tread.

These swans like the riddlic swan seem to touch the spiritual world and to
draw man home (inward and outward) with their winged calling.

Many birds have been proposed for the warbling minstrel of this riddle—
thrush, jay, chough, jackdaw, wood pigeon—but the night-singer and
song-shaper, bird of court and bode of joy, must be the *nightingale*. Pliny
says that the nightingale begins to sing when spring buds swell, shapes its
song with clever modulations, sustained notes, checks, murmurs, trills—
that it winds up and down—soprano, mezzo, baritone—like a bird of
many voices or a magical flute. Trained nightingales are said to compose
melodies, compete with their peers, even to recite poetry. The power and
beauty of the nightingale's song, mythical or real, is celebrated by English
poets, medieval and modern. Alcuin elegizes the bird whose "harmonies
grace its tiny throat," whose "heart-song raises the Creator's praise,"
whose "melody remains through night-shadow." Ten centuries later
Keats is still singing to the "light-winged Dryad of the trees / In some
melodious plot / Of beechen green, and shadows numberless" whose
song "of summer in full-throated ease" both enthralls and haunts the
poet ("Ode to a Nightingale"). The riddlic nightingale is a song-shaper
and world-charmer who is able to keep men bowed in a magical curve
while she sings with many voices the welcome-world into being. This
power as poet to capture and recreate an inner landscape in the listener's
mind is also emphasized by Gerard Manley Hopkins in the fifth verse of
"The Nightingale":

> For he began at once and shook
> My head to hear. He might have strung
> A row of ripples in the brook,
>   So forcibly he sung,
> The mist upon the leaves have strewed,
> And danced the balls of dew that stood
> In acres all above the wood.

Although as Hopkins notes, it is rightly the male bird that courts and sings,
in the riddle and much of the later poetry, it is the female who weaves
(round the male poet) a warbled spell in song.

The changeling who destroys its foster brothers and sisters is the *cuckoo*. Its bizarre craft and ungrateful behavior have made it a villain of the bird world. The mother cuckoo leaves her egg in the nest of another bird and by an evolutionary adaptation known as egg mimicry, fools the host mother into adopting the egg as her own. The hatched cuckoo, often stronger than its siblings, is skilled in ejecting both eggs and fledglings from the nest. Pliny notes that the greedy cuckoo seizes its siblings' food and grows so sleek and fat that the mother dotes on it, sometimes disowning her own starveling brood. According to myth the cuckoo responds ungratefully by bolting down not only the siblings but occasionally its mother as well. So Chaucer calls the cuckoo an "unkind" or unnatural bird, and Shakespeare draws upon the same tradition when in *I Henry IV* the Earl of Worcester laments Bolingbroke's unnatural usurpation of the throne:

> And, being fed by us, you used us so
> As that ungentle gull, the cuckoo's bird,
> Useth the sparrow—did oppress our nest;
> Grew by our feeding to so great a bulk
> That even our love durst not come near your sight
> For fear of swallowing.
>
> [5.1.59–64]

In Old English poetry the cuckoo is not only a harbinger of spring but a bode of sorrow. So the reflective traveler of "The Seafarer" says, pondering the passing of the world:

> The voice of the cuckoo, summer's lord,
> Sings of sorrow, bodes mourning—
> The heart's keen, sad song.

Orphan and marauder, the cuckoo passes on perverse love's claims in an alien world.

RIDDLE 8

The strange bird born of wood, wind, and wave is the *barnacle goose* which breeds in the Arctic and visits Britain in the winter. The bird was thought to be produced from a barnacle and even classified as a shellfish by some churchmen who enjoyed eating roast barnacle goose on fast days. Giraldus Cambrensis describes the bird in his twelfth-century *Topography of Ireland* (1.15):

> Barnacles are produced by nature in a strange manner. They look like marsh geese but are smaller. They first appear as gumlike growths on fir beams floating on the sea; then they hang down by their beaks from the wood like seaweed, locked in their shells to secure a free and steady growth. In time they are covered with a strong coat of feathers and either fall off into the sea or fly into the air. While attached to the timber they take their nourishment from the juices of the wet wood.

RIDDLE 9

This lovely, dangerous lady, like Keats's Lamia, seems "some demon's mistress, or the demon's self." She has been identified as *gold, night, wine* —even *night debauch*. Her gown of silver and garnet, her power to enfeeble or enrage men, and the reference to God's grim toast at the end of the riddle—all make *cup of wine or spirits* the probable solution. Like the lady "mead" of riddle 25 who is "binder and scourge of men," this seductress lures and lays out the strongest of warriors, stripping them of strength. There is a grim death-joke (something commonplace in much of early Nordic poetry) at the end of the riddle: As drunk fools continue to raise and praise the wine-cup which they take to be their "dearest treasure," grim God will raise, judge, and damn their souls (the real treasure) to an eternal drinking of hell's "dark woe in the dregs of pleasure." Tipplers may find this no happy wassail!

This is the first of three *ox* riddles in the Exeter Book. "Ox" riddles 10 and 36 are fashioned about the central paradox: Living, I break the land —dead, I bind man. Medieval Latin "ox" riddles by Aldhelm and Eusebius (see note to riddle 36) use the same motif. "Ox" riddle 70 is a narrative portrayal of the ox as a beast of burden. The ox of riddle 10 seems to hold a savage and sensuous power. Alive, it ravages the land in an act of regenerative plunder. Dead, it offers its supple skin as a pleasure to man. It brings wine to the warrior, binds and braces both lord and servant, arches up for the fierce-footed woman, and thrusts against the lecherous slave-girl who comes to warm, wet, and work over her lord's new skin. Whether this last bit of leather is shoe or shirt seems lost in the burgeoning sexual play of the riddle. The paradox is repeated with a twist at the end—for the "down land" has been endowed with its own sexuality. What the lady treads, the land also needs!

After much debate (and a variety of wild solutions such as *butterfly trans-formations, alphabet letters,* and *ten fingers*), critics have settled on *ten chickens* as the solution to this riddle. The house of each chicken is a shell with a filament skin or membrane hung on the inside wall. The six brothers and four sisters remain something of a problem: the best guess to date is that Old English *ten ciccenu,* a Northumbrian dialect spelling for "ten chickens," contains six consonants and four vowels—though this seems overly ingenious to some.

This is the first of several *horn* riddles in the Exeter Book. This riddle and riddle 76 describe musical and drinking horns; riddles 84 and 89 describe inkhorns; riddle 26, a possible wooden trumpet made of yew. The animal weapon—stripped by a hunter, adorned by a smith, borne to battle by a grim lord or to table by a serving lady—may be an aurochs horn similar to the two discovered at Sutton Hoo. The now extinct aurochs was a large, long-horned wild ox hunted by the Germanic tribes. In his *Gallic War* (6.28), Caesar says that the bullish animals ("only slightly smaller than elephants") were trapped in pits and slain, their horns cut, carved, and tipped in silver to be used as beakers at great banquets. Such horns were a sign of prowess and wealth. They were also an invitation to hard drinking because they would not stand upright on the table (once filled they had to be quaffed!). The horn is thus war-weapon and hall-joy: its song bodes wassail or slaughter—and sometimes at the banquet table of feuding families a grim mixture of both.

RIDDLE 13

The savage protectress of this riddle, a woodland Kali, continues to be the subject of some debate. Candidates include the *badger, porcupine, hedgehog, fox,* and *weasel.* All bear battle-weapons (tooth, claw, or spine), but the coloring and quick canter, furred cheeks and high ears, fit only the fox. This grassland loper lives in a burrow dug with its forepaws or borrowed from a badger (foxes often steal and enlarge other creatures' dens). The vixen is known to be a passionate mother and fierce defender of her young. Her natural enemy is the dog, called a "slaughter-hound" in the riddle; and also in Anglo-Saxon times, the wolf. Threatened by the snuffling death-door intruder, her first thought is for her children. Having secured her young, she leads the stalker through tight burrow tunnels and lures him out her back door (Grimsgate) where she turns to offer him an unexpected feast of battle-tooth and war-claw. The riddlic she-fox is no storied Reynard, no wily actor in the cultivated chase of men—she slaughters the civilized dog. A similar power and aura characterize the vixen in Adrienne Rich's poem, "Abnegation" (from *Leaflets*), which begins:

> The red fox, the vixen
> dancing in the half-light among the junipers,
> wise-looking in a sexy way,

Egyptian-supple in her sharpness—
what does she want
with the dreams of dead vixens,
the apotheosis of Reynard,
the literature of fox-hunting?
Only in her nerves the past
sings, a thrill of self-preservation.
I go along down the road
to a house nailed together by Scottish
Covenanters, instinct mortified
in a virgin forest,
and she springs toward her den
every hair on her pelt alive
with tidings of the immaculate present.

RIDDLE 14

This storm-battler guarding its treasure against wind and wave is an *anchor*.
The riddle shares some themes with the fifth-century Latin riddle of
Symphosius:

My twin points are bound by an iron bar.
I wrestle with wind, struggle with the sea.
I probe deep waters—I bite the earth.

Both the anchor and the elements seem more animated in the storm and
strife of the Old English riddle. Like an epic warrior, the Saxon anchor
seizes glory in the pitch of war. Against its enemies, wind and wave, it holds
its floating hoard with the help of the stones' clutch.

RIDDLE 15

This strange weapon-gobbler and spear-spitter which sounds like some
Anglo-Saxon version of the Trojan horse has never been satisfactorily identified. Some think it is a Roman *ballista* or *catapult* (the Anglo-Saxons

had no such weapon, though they might have read about it) or a Saxon *sling*, but spears and arrows would hardly have been shot from such contrivances. One possibility, a *fortress*, might be full of old weapon-treasures, though its belly hardly "bound by wires." Another suggestion is *forge*—though one might expect riddlic mention of heating, hammering, cooling, and quenching in such a riddle. Another more metaphoric solution is *inkwell* with its dangerous pens darting in and out—but the creature seems too demonstrably murderous for such a tame solution. A *weapon chest* might swallow, hold, and even (with poetic license) "spit forth" spears, arrows, and other treasures—but the riddlic tone and imagery suggests that the creature is more an engaged battle-warrior than a detached house-servant. Surely the right solution to this riddle remains to be found.

RIDDLE 16

The few remaining clues of this fragment point to a broad-bellied container of some sort used in the shipping trade—probably an *amphora* or large pottery jug often associated with the continental wine trade. These amphorae, whose remains are found in Anglo-Saxon digs, were as large as three or four feet in height.

RIDDLE 17

This is one of two similarly structured, runic *ship* riddles in the Exeter Book (the other is riddle 62). Each plays upon the common Old English kenning of the ship as sea-horse. The nailed horse (ship) sails a smooth plain (sea), carrying a hawk (sail) and a man (sailor). In this riddle the runes—represented by capital letters in the translation—must be reversed to spell out the clues: HORSE, MAN, HERO, HAWK. For a time the runic clues were thought to constitute the solution, "A man upon horseback with a hawk on his fist," or to point to *falconry* as a general solution—but this seems little more than a restatement of the literal clues. The nailed horse of the fierce-flowing road must be a nailed clinker ship of the sort unearthed at Sutton Hoo. Another ingenious (though finally less likely) solution recently put forward is that the nailed horse is a hand bearing a hawklike quill in the journey of pen and ink across the page—thus the solution, *writing.*

The slaughtering treasure of this riddle is a *sword,* though other solutions like *sword-swallow (hawk)* and the little-death dealing *phallus* have also been proposed. The sword celebrates its ominous splendor, the glint of death, then cuts through court-praise to its savage description of killing battle-foe and even bench-friend. Because of the latter danger, the Anglo-Saxons levied fines against the unsheathed sword at the mead-hall table. In the world of *Beowulf,* the sword is often a symbol of the feud and a spur to vengeance. The riddlic sword has its own mock-feud with its lord's ungrateful wife who prefers the power and pleasure of its fertile double, the implied phallus. Beginning at line 16, the riddle turns on this elaborate conceit. The celibate steel brings real death to men, not the little death that women love. If the sword battles well, it begets no children; if it fails on the field, it is sent to the smithy to be melted down and reforged into the next generation of weapons. In contrast, the phallic sword that the wife loves engenders life as it thrusts and parries. The battle-sword that serves well is a celibate killer; the phallic sword that serves, seeds life. The riddlic conceit of the two swords with their competing worlds finds a mirror image at the end of John Donne's "Elegy: Love's War":

> Here let me war; in these arms let me lie;
> Here let me parley, batter, bleed, and die.
> Thine arms imprison me, and mine arms thee;
> Thy heart thy ransom is; take mine for me.
> Other men war that they their rest may gain,
> But we will rest that we may fight again.
> Those wars the ignorant, these the experienced love;

There we are always under, here above.
There engines far off breed a just true fear;
Near thrusts, pikes, stabs, yea bullets hurt not here.
There lies are wrongs, here safe uprightly lie.
There men kill men; we'll make one by and by.
Thou nothing; I not half so much shall do
In these wars as they may which from us two
Shall spring. Thousands we see which travel not
To wars, but stay—swords, arms, and shot
To make at home. And shall not I do then
More glorious service, staying to make men?

One real sword, one metaphoric—one to kill, one to engender life: in bringing the two together, the mind itself a blade between the sheer worlds of love and death, of blood spilled and spirit seeded.

RIDDLE 19

This strange ground-skulker is an Anglo-Saxon *plow*, its dagger and sword the colter and share. The plow is drawn by the "dark enemy of forests" —presumably the ox that has uprooted trees and turned woodlands to fields. It is driven by a "bent lord"—the farmer who in Anglo-Saxon society may be either freeman or slave. The lot of the Anglo-Saxon farmer is described in Aelfric's *Colloquy:*

> My work is hard. I rise at daybreak, drive oxen to the field, and yoke them to the plow. No winter weather is too keen for me— I cannot stay home for fear of my lord. When I've yoked the oxen and fastened the colter and share to the plow, I must plow at least an acre a day. . . . A boy helps me drive by goading the oxen, but he is hoarse with the shouting and cold. . . . I also must fill the ox-stalls with hay, bring in water and carry off dung. . . . It's a hard life because I'm a slave.

Paradoxically the "driving lord" of the riddle must also "slave well."

For many years this riddle was solved as the *month of December,* with its half-days (or days and nights) the sixty warriors on horseback riding from the shore of the old year to that of the new. The eleven special horses were thought to be December's four bright Sundays and seven feast days. But the fact that December has thirty-one days (sixty-two riders?) and often five Sundays (some of them occasionally feast days) presents problems. Recently a new solution has been proposed—*Charles's Wain and the circling stars.* The wagon which carries horses and riders from the horizon's shore up over the dangerous sea of the sky and back again is the constellation, Charles's Wain. The eleven special riders are thought to be the stars of Canes Venatici (just under the Wain), four of them quite bright. The "sixty" riders are thought to represent merely a "multitude" of circling stars according to a briefly documented medieval tradition. It must be admitted that neither of the solutions explains without some forcing the choice of numbers in the riddle or the detailed attention given to the description of the tumultuous sea. Can you guess what the collocation of sixty, eleven, and four might mean?

This twisted killer's name is Wob—*bow* backwards. The Germanic bow was a weapon of both war and the chase. In *Beowulf,* for example, when the Geats reach Grendel's mere, they hunt the lake monsters with bows and arrows (1430 ff.):

> Lake-dragons and wild things fell back
> Heart-bitter when they heard the war-horn wail.
> A warrior of the Geats separated one
> From the battle-surge with a death-bow
> So the strife-arrow stood in his heart:
> He was a slow swimmer in the death-grip.

Battle-bows and arrows as death-dealers are often metonymic symbols for death itself, as in Wiglaf's eulogy for Beowulf (3114 ff.):

Dark flames will drink, devour the prince
Of warriors who long withstood war-storm,
Iron-rain, the sharp wind of arrows shot
Over shield-walls, driven by bow-strings:
Shaft served barb, death-feathers whistling.

The riddlic bow is a wizard-warrior: When bent with the battle-sting in its belly, it is not dying (as a man might be) but priming to murder. It spits what it swallows—the whistling snake, the death-drink. The venomous cup hearkens back to the Devil's death-feast in the Garden of Eden. Man's fallen legacy seems symbolized by the bow. Bound, it serves its warlord properly—but murderously in a world of vengeance.

RIDDLE 22

In the Old English text of this riddle, runes spell out the bird's name, "higora," which I have translated as *magpie* with my corresponding (mixed up) capitals—though another possible translation is *jay*. Both birds, closely related, are well-known mimics and saucy janglers. The pie's ability to imitate animals and men—almost as if shifting shapes—has given it a demonic reputation. In medieval Scotland it was known as the Devil's bird. Beryl Rowland notes that the magpie "was said to have been the only bird which refused to enter the Ark, preferring instead to perch on the roof and gabble over the drowning world" (*Birds with Human Souls*, p. 102). Perhaps the pie of this riddle is not so foreboding as the legendary trickster, but its shape-shifting song does haunt in an eerie way.

RIDDLE 23

This is one of several Old English double-entendre riddles with a sexual solution for the bawdy and a plain solution for the prim. On the kitchen-counter carving-bed, the lady lays an *onion*. Back in the bedroom—another bulb and skin. The onion begins its "Song of Myself" with a litany of power, but after the entrance of the Achillic woman, eager-armed and proud, the "I" fractures into body, head, and skin—as the lady grabs, rushes, holds, and claims. The power struggle is resolved in the paradox of the fast catch, the mutual delight of "our meeting," and the oblique conclusion (the enactment of "something to come"). The phallic onion links the green world with the world of human sexuality. Nature is charged with human metaphor; passion is charted with natural myth.

RIDDLE 24

This *Bible* or *book* riddle is probably the earliest sustained piece of book-art poetry in English. A number of Latin riddles treat the same subject—among them the "parchment" riddles of Tatwine and Eusebius, two eighth-century English churchmen:

> A fierce robber ripped off my hide,
> Plundered the breath-pores of my skin.
> I was shaped by an artist and author
> Into a flat field. Furrowed and wet,
> I yield strange fruit. My meadows bloom
> Food for the healthy, health for the sick.

*   *   *

> Once silent, voiceless, wordless, dumb—
> Now voiceless, silent, bearing words we come,
> White fields crossed by myriad black tracks:
> Alive we are dumb—dead, answer back.

The Old English riddle celebrates in longer, more lyrical fashion the life of the parchment from beast to book. The Bible suffers its own form of passion as it is ripped, stretched, scraped, cut, and scratched by the quill ("the bird's once wind-stiff joy"); but as keeper and conveyor of the Word, it transcends its fate to bring grace, honor, and glory to men. Its inner treasure is reflected in its outer appearance—multicolored illuminations, gold leaf, and a jeweled cover. The process of making the medieval manuscript was a long and arduous one linking the talents of leather-worker, artist, scribe, and poet—as is clear in the following tenth-century description of manuscript preparation by a monk of Saint Gallen:

> I cut the parchment for my lord's books,
> Rub it with pumice and lift off dross,
> Line it with a stylus and straight rule,
> Labor over letters with a long point,
> Yoke the painter's passion—figures grand
> And fine—smooth and fasten it for my lord:
> A writer's delight and a reader's joy.

RIDDLE 25

This powerful creature is *mead* made from honey, a favorite Anglo-Saxon drink. The number of "mead-" compounds in Old English attests to its central place in the culture. Comrades come to the mead-hall on the mead-path, sit at mead-benches drinking from mead-cups and getting mead-high until they drop, mead-weary. All this in a gay city called a mead-burg. When Beowulf returns home from monster-killing in Denmark, he and his troop are made welcome in proper meadish fashion (1975 ff.):

> The mead-hall was cleared as the king ordered,
> Mead-benches readied for the marching men.
> The survivor sat down, kinsman with kinsman,
> Beowulf with his king, after he greeted
> With ceremonial speech his liege-lord.
> Haereth's daughter, Hygelac's queen,
> Who loved and served her proud people,
> Passed through the high hall bearing mead-cups,
> Powerful drink to the hands of war-men.
> . . . .
> There was joy in the troop, more than man's

Measure under heaven's arch: hall-thanes
Held mead-mirth.

But the drinking could sour and the vengeful spirit erupt as the riddle implies, so weapons were often forbidden at the mead-hall table. The dangerous effect of drink on a war-man's mind is aptly described in "The Fortunes of Men":

> Sometimes the sword's edge steals the life
> Of an ale-drinker or a wine-weary man
> At the mead-bench. His words are too quick.
> Another drinks beer from the cup-bearer's hand,
> Grows drunk as a mead-fool, forgets to check
> His mouth with his mind, seeks suffering,
> A long life's end, a joyless hall.
> Men name him the mead-wild self-slayer.

The riddlic mead also seizes power, binding and laying low young and old alike. The central paradox of mead is this: Helpless to withstand man's plundering and processing, it is transformed into a mighty agent that enters man's home (and head!) to render its conqueror helpless.

R I D D L E 26

This riddle was long solved as *John Barleycorn* or *beer* but the traditional solution has recently come under hard scrutiny. Barley is not hard and fierce unless its bristles are taken as spears. Beer needs mashing, boiling, and fermenting—none of which is mentioned in the process verbs of lines 3–5. These verbs might fit the fashioning of barrel staves in a *wine cask*, but this solution, like "beer," does not fit the musical terms at the end of the riddle. Three instruments have been suggested: *harp (lyre)*, *tortoise shell lyre*, and *horn of yew*. All of these fit the central paradox of the riddle (which is also found in several Latin riddles on musical instruments): Living, it is silent—dead, it sings. The tortoise lyre, though a classical instrument, was neither known nor played in Anglo-Saxon England. The Old English lyre was made of maple, which is not the hardest or fiercest of woods. The hard, fierce killer of the opening lines might be the yew, hardest of Anglo-Saxon woods whose needlelike leaves contain the alkaloid poison responsible for its grim reputation. The hard wood might be carved and shaped into a long horn in the fashion described in lines 3–5 and borne to the hall to produce its clarion joy. Irish horns of this sort have been discovered and the existence of a similarly made English wooden horn seems likely. A more recent solution is *damascened sword.* The riddlic verbs of lines 3–5 fit neatly the pattern-welding process (various iron rods are twisted, shaped, and forged to produce a hard steel). In this case the initial lines must be taken to describe jointly the original ore's homeland and the ultimate steel's fierce strength. The musical imagery must be toned down at the end of the riddle and slain swordsmen made to sing a different tune after death instead of the creature itself. The Old English riddle has a number of textual, grammatical, and semantic ambiguities which makes manipulation in support of each of the solutions possible. My own translation reflects a fairly common bias that the creature is a musical instrument of sorts.

RIDDLE 27

This riddle describes an imaginary conflict between *moon and sun.* A few days before new moon, a waning sliver rises, stealing its strand of light from the sun (the Anglo-Saxons believed both moon and stars reflected sunlight). This "curved lamp of the air" fetches home to its night-chamber another booty of pale light (sometimes called by sailors "the old moon in the arms of the new") which the riddler saw but could only describe in metaphoric terms. Modern science has taught us that this pale image of the full moon is actually earthlight, light reflected from earth to moon. The crescent-moon marauder plots to keep this light-treasure in its sky-castle. But dawn appears and the pale treasure disappears, retaken by the sun. As the sun becomes visible, the moon itself pales, then disappears over the horizon. Like a righteous warrior, the sun has successfully reclaimed its light. The next night (new moon), the plundering moon has disappeared, and groundlings wonder where the wanderer has gone. In a few days the cycle will begin again with the waxing sliver.

RIDDLE 28

This is the only riddle in the Exeter Book for which there are two texts, collated here for purposes of translation. The slightly damaged variant occurs immediately preceding riddle 58 in the manuscript and shows only minor differences. There has been much critical debate about this riddle, though most editors agree that its solution is *tree* or *wood*. There is a double irony at the heart of the riddle: the living tree (lines 1–4) endures the natural threat of fire and storm but succumbs to man—then cut and crafted (lines 5–9) into cup or cross, it is loved and worshiped by hall-thanes. Whether the last lines refer to the holy cross or the demonic cup (compare the enchantress wine-cup of riddle 9) may be a moot point. Whatever its cultural uses and symbolic value in man's world, it has as an art object returned to power. Bloom-wood before, it now enables man to bloom—with religious bliss or a wassail buzz.

RIDDLE 29

The slung-up bird is a *bagpipe*—and this riddle is one of the earliest known descriptions of the strange musical instrument. Like a canny shaper or dream-singer, the bird plays mute—her beak (chanter) hung down and her hands and feet (drones and mouthpiece) slung up. Helpless but song-hungry, she is passed round the hall and pressed to sing. She drinks no mead but a bellyful of air—her hoard. Jeweled and naked, she sings through her dangling legs—makes melody with her chanter while the drones ride dangling from their glory-sister's neck. While her shape is strange, her song is sublime—she transforms the plain hall of earls into a dream world of dance and song. Handled with craft and shaped with wind—with breath and skill she shapes song.

RIDDLE 30

This one-footed monster from the workshops of men that sails on the smooth plain is a *ship*. Strangely misshapen, with a belly full of food for the disgorging, she slides onto the shore. The merchant's imported haul in Aelfric's *Colloquy* includes "purple cloth and silks, precious gems and gold, rare garments and herbs, spices and perfumes, wine and oil, ivory and bronze, copper and tin, sulphur and glass," but the ship of this riddle carries "corn-gold, grain-treasure, wine-wealth." Like the bread of "oven" riddle 47, these are the "sustaining treasures dearer than gold . . . sought by kings, queens, and princes / For benefit and pleasure."

RIDDLE 31

This is the first of two *iceberg* riddles in the collection; the other is riddle 66. Normally icebergs are not found in British waters, but occasional erratics that wander from their recognized paths of travel have been sighted in the vicinity of the British Isles. These have apparently drifted eastward from northeast Greenland via the East Iceland current. Similar erratics of the eighth or ninth century were probably within sailing range of Anglo-Saxon sailors such as King Alfred's Ohthere. In the riddle the iceberg is depicted as a beautiful but dangerous woman-warrior armed with ice-blades and a ready curse. The riddle-within-a-riddle of the last five lines has as its solution, *water*. Water is the mother of ice and also its daughter (pregnant again with potential ice). For another literary sailor's view of the cold death-stalker, compare the last lines of Herman Melville's "The Berg":

> Hard Berg (methought), so cold, so vast,
> With mortal damps self-overcast;
> Exhaling still thy dankish breath—
> Adrift dissolving, bound for death;
> Though lumpish thou, a lumbering one—
> A lumbering lubbard loitering slow,

Impingers rue thee and go down,
Sounding thy precipice below,
Nor stir the slimy slug that sprawls
Along thy dead indifference of walls.

RIDDLE 32

This virtuous ground-dogger, plant-scratcher, crop-catcher is not some
weird pooch but an Anglo-Saxon *rake*. It noses, scruffs, and plunders
weeds, thins gardens and fields for a crop of fair flowers and good grain.
The tone, a curious mixture of mock heroic and pastoral joy, is reminiscent of Thoreau's crop-care and weed-attacks in "The Bean-Field" of
Walden.

RIDDLE 33

This *coat of mail* or *byrnie* riddle is a close translation of a Latin riddle
by the seventh-century English churchman Aldhelm. Two versions of the
Old English riddle exist—one the West Saxon version in the Exeter
Book, the other a Northumbrian version in a Leiden University Library
collection of Latin riddles. The mail shirt defines itself here mainly by
negatives: it is not made by the traditional weaving process (for a discussion of the Anglo-Saxon loom, see the note to riddle 54). Chain-mail was
formed from iron rings welded together by a skilled smith. Although few
Anglo-Saxon byrnies have been found in the archaeological sites, they do
play a large part in the traditional war poetry. The arrival of Beowulf's
band to Hrothgar's Heorot is announced by the glint and song of mail
(321 ff.):

> Their war-corselets shone, hard and hand-locked
> (The glittering ring-iron groaned in battle)—
> Grim guests came to the hall in war-gear.

And Beowulf greets Hrothgar in his likewise glittering cloak (405):

Beowulf spoke—on his body chain-mail shone,
A war-net woven, sewn by a skilled smith.

But chain-mail is not worn merely as a show stopper—it has a useful battlefield function. When Beowulf dives down to Grendel's lair, he is careful to don his protective shirt (1441 ff.):

Beowulf put on warrior's clothes, life-linked.
His chain-mail—hard, broad, hand-woven—
Would breach the sea: it knew how to keep
The bone-house whole so his fierce foe's
Hand-crush could not reach his heart.

Like jeweled swords, Anglo-Saxon mail-coats were heirlooms of great value worn only by leaders and lords. Ordinary soldiers probably wore leather jerkins on the battlefield.

RIDDLE 34

This riddle offers a surrealistic scene with its mixture of wings, heads, hands, and feet. Are the shapes of horse, man, dog, bird, and woman real or metaphoric apparitions? One riddle editor in a fit of despair wishes the riddle "at the bottom of the Bay of Portugal [for] there is no poetry in it, and the ingenuity is misplaced." The craft is taken by most to be a *ship*, though the nature of the creatures is a matter of debate. My own guess is that the four feet under the ship's belly are oars; the eight feet above belong to four oarsmen. The wings are sails; the twelve eyes and six heads belong to the four oarsmen and two figureheads fore and aft. The boat leaves one track. The shape of the horse is the ship itself ("sea-horse" is a common kenning for "ship") with its birdlike sail. The man is a sailor. The likeness of the dog and the face of a woman may describe the figure-heads (female and animal heads may be seen on ships in the Bayeux Tapestry). Similar motifs may be found in "ship" riddles 17 and 62 and in riddle 72, possibly a "ship's figurehead." The bizarre quality of the riddle is reminiscent of certain neck-riddles (for an example of this genre, see riddle 82).

This is the bawdy *bellows* riddle—the plain one occurs at riddle 83. Here the hard-muscled man labors over air at the forge fire while his double struggles with the pump of love. The creature fills, gorges, spills, dies and rises with another "breath." It sires a son—air or child—and fathers a newly engorged self. The potent play on death and the resurrection embraces sacred, profane, and passionate worlds. In this the riddler seems a budding metaphysical poet.

RIDDLE 36

This is one of three *ox* riddles in the Exeter Book—its solution is *young ox* or *bull calf.* It shares with riddle 70 the theme of the four fountains; and with riddle 10 the central paradox: Living I break the land—dead I bind man. Riddle 10 highlights the sensuality of leather; riddle 70 concentrates on the theme of the ox as suffering servant. This riddle with its colloquial language, its prescient country bystander, and its natural celebration of Bess and boy, seems wrought with the tone and humor of a Saxon Frost. The English "ox" riddles share common motifs with two Latin "ox" riddles—the first by the seventh-century English churchman Aldhelm, who was Bishop of Sherborne late in life, the second by the eighth-century English Abbot Eusebius of Wearmouth:

> Down a dry throat I drink from four
> Foaming fountains—gulping, sucking.
> With life-strength I break the downs,
> Root stumps, crack clay, rip soil.
> When the life-breath leaves my cold limbs,
> I bind mighty men with strong thongs.

> *   *   *

> After my mother has brought me birth,
> I gulp four streams from one spring.

Living I begin to break the land—
Dead I bind the living man.

RIDDLE 37

This riddle, a strange symphony of paradoxes, continues to perplex and
delight its readers. The riddler taunts us with his claim that writings reveal
the creature's plain presence among men. We should know it—it seeks
each living person, moves everywhere in the wide world, and carries comfort to the children of middle-earth. Yet its power passes knowing. No
wonder—it has no hands, feet, mouth, mind, or soul. Yet it lives. It is the
poorest of creatures, yet it reaps glory. It is marvelously difficult to catch
with words, yet everything said about it is true. What do the riddle solvers
say? The most tangible solutions are *moon, cloud,* and *day.* But none of
these can lay proper claim to the riddle-creature's mysterious movement
and power. Better guesses are *time, death, speech,* and *dream.* These are
with us, bound up in our living, too close perhaps to be recognized. None
of the solutions, however, satisfies wholly the paradoxical demands of the
riddle. Can it be that the creature closest to us remains to be discovered?
"It has no limbs, yet it lives!" What is it?

RIDDLE 38

This *nature* or *creation* riddle is based on a long Latin original by the
seventh-century English churchman Aldhelm, who composed a "century," or set of one hundred Latin riddles. The Old English riddler ex-
panded and reshaped portions of the Latin to make a leaner (some would
say thinner) style; my own translation is a somewhat condensed version of
the Old English. The riddle celebrates what the Anglo-Saxons called "forð-
gesceaft," "creation-bodying-forth," or the divine and discernible spirit
infused in all things. Gerard Manley Hopkins, himself a medievalist of
sorts, called this *inscape,* "the dearest freshness deep down things,"
which makes our world "flame out like shining from shook foil" ("God's

Grandeur"). For Hopkins, as for the riddler I think, this shining forth is both a song of self—

> Each mortal thing does one thing and the same:
> Deals out that being indoors each one dwells;
> Selves—goes itself; *myself* it speaks and spells—

and the supreme embodiment of God: for each one

> Acts in God's eye what in God's eye he is—
> Christ. For Christ plays in ten thousand places. . . .
> ["As Kingfishers Catch Fire"]

This divine and natural selving is reminiscent, in the American tradition, of Whitman's *Song of Myself* where the poet celebrates "God in every object" (stanza 48). Whitman's catalogic yoking of the great and small is often like that of the riddle. For example, in stanza 31, Whitman sings:

> I believe a leaf of grass is no less than the journey-work of the
>   stars,
> And the pismire is equally perfect, and a grain of sand, and the
>   egg of the wren,
> And the tree-toad is a chef-d'œuvre for the highest,
> And the running blackberry would adorn the parlors of heaven.

The sense of this shaping spirit—ancient and always becoming—locked in the largest and smallest, lightest and darkest, fiercest and feeblest of creatures is also reminiscent of William Blake's notion of the "Infinite in all things" best captured in the opening lines of "Auguries of Innocence":

> To see a World in a Grain of Sand
> And a Heaven in a Wild Flower,
> Hold Infinity in the palm of your hand
> And Eternity in an hour.

In the Old English riddle the spirit of creation is broader than the earth, smaller than a handworm, older than the universe, younger than yesterday's child. In its infinite aspect it sings: "I weave round the world a glittering cloak / A *kind* embrace"—this is the gift of grace and a natural shaping (each *kind* has its own shaping, selving). Creation shapes and sustains the world—it is the sun's grandeur and the beetle's dung. The reference to the mythical pernex in line 44 is a mistranslation of the Latin *plus pernix aquilis*, "swifter than the eagle."

RIDDLE 39

This fragment may be part of a longer *water* riddle—for the water-creature at riddle 80 is similarly described as the "mother of many well-known creatures" whose "lineage sings the spawn of creation." Two other sustaining mothers might be possible solutions—*earth* and *nature*.

RIDDLE 40

Bedroom carousers and barnyard hands may know from experience these bawdy birds. Bookworms will have to unravel the capital clue of the central lines. The letters (runic names in the original text) rearranged spell COCK and HEN. The cock is often associated with proud lechery in the Middle Ages. Chaucer's Chauntecleer feathers Pertelote twenty times before nine in the morning and prowls up and down the barnyard like a grim lion. Housebroken cocks are similarly affected. This is clear in a riddlelike fifteenth-century lyric which begins in the barnyard and ends in the bedroom:

> I have a gentle cock
> That crows and sings my day:
> He makes me rise up early
> My sweet matins to say.
>
> I have a gentle cock
> Who comes of stock so great:

His comb is of red coral,
His tail is of jet.

I have a gentle cock
Whose line is straight and true;
His comb is of red coral,
His tail an indigo blue.

His light legs are of azure,
So gentle and so small;
His foot-spurs are of silver-white
Up to the root and nail.

His eyes are set like crystal
Locked up in amber,
And every night he perches high
In my lady's chamber.

Like the song, the riddle ends on a sexual twist. The heart of the riddle is love's stronghold unlocked with a literate or libidinous key. Scholars will take sublimated pleasure in discovering the solution. Common carousers will simply enjoy the low-down fun.

RIDDLE 41

The lordly guest of great lineage is the *soul;* its servant and brother, the *body.* Earth is mother and sister to both: mother because the whole man, body and soul, was shaped from clay; sister because earth, soul, and body were all formed by the same father, God. The body must serve the soul in liege-lord fashion, but each must love and care for the other as a brother because finally they are bound in judgment. Damnation will bring them a progeny of woe when, like an unhappy couple, they suffer the torments of hell. Or united in salvation on the Judgment Day, they may bask in the bliss of heaven. The riddle itself may be sire to a lasting "soul and body" lyric tradition in English poetry. There are two versions of a long soul and body poem in Old English; in the longer of the two a damned soul returns to revile, and a saved soul to praise, its earthly servant. In Middle English there is a lengthy, acrimonious debate between soul and body over who is to blame for their shared damnation. Shakespeare uses the soul and body motif in "Sonnet 146" ("Poor soul, the center of my sinful earth"), and Andrew Marvell plays with a final, ironic twist upon the earlier debate tradition in his "Dialogue between the Soul and Body." For a modern treatment of the tradition, see William Butler Yeats's "A Dialogue of Self and Soul."

RIDDLE 42

This is the first of two *key* riddles in the Exeter collection—the other less bawdy rendering is riddle 87. The key itself may dangle on a belt beneath the Anglo-Saxon tunic; its lascivious twin is also hung boldly beneath and below. The small miracle may open love's lock as it slips snugly into the "hole it has long come to fill." The pun on "long" (a habitual action, an attained length) is playfully present in the Old English. This is certainly the earliest English example of the sexual lock-and-key symbolism noted by Freud in his chapter on the dreamwork (6.E) in *The Interpretation of Dreams*.

RIDDLE 43

For polite company the answer to this riddle is *bread dough*—though lustier spirits may find the phallic solution barely concealed. As in other double-entendre riddles, the poet is at pains to keep both solutions before us, teasing us with what sometimes seems a riddlic Rorschach Test. In playful fashion the riddle is also an elaborate and punningly obscene etymological joke since the Old English word for "lord" means literally "guardian of the loaf," and the word for "lady," literally "kneader of the dough." The lady in question is presumably making more than cakes.

Notes and Commentary

191

This complicated kinship riddle whose solution is *Lot and his family* is based on the story of Lot's incest in Genesis 19. Lot's family is warned by two angels to leave the wicked city of Sodom and not to look back on its devastation. In flight Lot's wife disobeys, looks back, and is turned to a pillar of salt. Lot wanders off with his two daughters to live in a cave in the hills. Lot's daughters despair of ever finding husbands and conspire with the help of a little wine to seduce their father. The Old English poetic "Genesis" (2600 ff.) describes the seduction with irony and pathos:

> Each sister took to her drunk father's bed,
> And the wise old man whose heart and head
> Were bound with wine saw wives not daughters:
> His mind was locked—and they were pregnant
> With the proud sons of their own dear father.
> The elder's was Moab, the younger's Ben-ammi.
> Scriptures say the two princes fathered nations.

The Old English riddle is based on the resulting confusion of kinship terms. Lot's wives are also his daughters; his sons are their sons and also his grandsons. Mothers and sons together, since they are all Lot's children, are also brothers and sisters. This makes each son paradoxically both uncle and nephew of the other. Midrash tradition has it that this impossible riddle was the second query proposed by the Queen of Sheba to Solomon to test his wisdom.

The thief who swallows songs is a *bookworm*. The riddler pokes mock-heroic fun at the pedantic worm, transformed into word-wolf or midnight marauder, who devours the substance without the spirit. The idea is based on the fifth-century Latin riddle of Symphosius:

I feed on words without knowing.
I live in books without learning.
I devour Muses without improving.

But the Old English riddle is also a lament for things past. The oral tradition of the singer has been supplanted by the literary conjunction of poet, missionary, and scribe. The old form of memory, the rhythmical word-hoard, has given way to the material storehouse of the vellum page. What the mind of the singer guarded and passed on, the book makes plain and perishable. The voiceless word is ravaged by time and the worm. What is left is a ruin. The theme is echoed by William Carlos Williams in the third book of *Paterson:*

> We read: not the flames
> but the ruin left
> by the conflagration
>
> Not the enormous burning
> but the dead (the books
> remaining). Let us read
>
> and digest: the surface
> glistens, only the surface.
> Dig in—and you have
>
> a nothing, surrounded by
> a surface, an inverted
> bell resounding, a
>
> white-hot man become
> a book, the emptiness of
> a cavern resounding

For Williams, as for the riddler, written words are ruins, voice-shards left on the page. The fire that gave rise to the vision must be rekindled, the song resung. The resounding space of the inverted bell is like the catalytic space of the riddle solver shaping the word-wolf out of the worm, waiting for the beast to sing. In the metaphor is the key to becoming other. The bookworm devours dead words in a ruin of substance without spirit. What the riddler dares us to do is to devour, substantiate, and sing.

RIDDLE 46

This creature, crafted of gold, whose inscription sings silently to the supplicant, must be one of the sacred vessels of the Mass—probably *paten* or *chalice*. The circle or "ring" ("anything round" in Old English) which holds its own sacred riddle, the blood-wine and embodied host of Christ, sings the supplicant's plea, urging man to partake of the deeper mystery of the Catholic faith. In carrying the symbolic form of Christ and in singing the supplicant's song, the creature itself mediates between man and God. For a more detailed treatment of the chalice, see riddle 57.

RIDDLE 47

What are the treasures "dearer than gold" swallowed by the creature and sought by man each day to sustain him? Probably books or bread. *Bookcase* and *oven* are thus the likeliest candidates for the deaf and dumb gulper (though *falcon cage* and *pen* have also been suggested). If the sustenance is metaphorical (wisdom), the bookcase shelves it; if literal (food or bread), the oven bakes it. The race of shapers may be scribes or cooks—each has its own enabling measure.

RIDDLE 48

The warrior is *fire*—its dumb parents, flint and steel. Scourge and protector, helpmate and hearth-devil—it serves well when ruled with a firm hand and hard mind. Without discipline and care, it grows wild and brings fools a grim reward. Measured, it serves; measureless, reaps!

The four weird fellows on the gold-plated road are a *quill pen and fingers* (or thumb with two supporting fingers). The brash bird, reduced to a feather, darts from inkwell to vellum road and back again. The road is rich with parchment gold. The motifs of the riddle are echoed in a number of medieval Latin riddles, among them a "quill" riddle by Tatwine, an eighth-century Archbishop of Canterbury:

> An enemy has seized, stolen my nature,
> For once I darted through the high air—
> Now bound by three, I pay a price on earth:
> I am forced to plow smooth, flat fields
> As love's labor drives me to weep
> Dark tears on dry furrows.

The two hard captives bound together as one punishing creature, wielded by a Welshwoman and slave, are probably the handle and swiple of a threshing *flail*. The Anglo-Saxon flail consisted of a wooden staff or handle with a short, stout, swinging club or swiple attached. Other possible solutions to the riddle include *broom, well buckets,* and *yoke of oxen.* The dark slave who ironically wields power in the poem is a Welshwoman, one of the descendants of the Britons who held power in Britain before the coming of the Anglo-Saxons. Since the Welsh were often enslaved, the word *Welshman* came to mean "slave" in Old English.

Like the spear of riddle 71 and the cross of "The Dream of the Rood," this tree-creature is ripped from its home in the forest, carried off and crafted by man into a murderous war-weapon. Bound by iron it becomes a mighty *battering ram* which clears the way through wooden walls for another fierce, swift warrior—man. Together these two blast and travel the grim road of battle—far from the tree's original joy in the blooming wood. This is a dark form of pastoral: what nature nurtures, man transforms into an instrument of war. No savage wind blows through the wild pines —the fiercest riddlic rush comes in the storm of battle.

RIDDLE 52

Like the earlier sexual, double-entendre "bread" and "onion" riddles (23 and 43), this one also has ostensibly to do with food. The male servant thrusts his plunger into the female *churn*—together they make the baby, butter. The riddle opens with a burst of machismo, slightly surreal in its ravishing treatment of the passive woman in the corner. The man has the action—he steps, lifts, thrusts (his "something" is mock modesty), and works his will. Yet the paradox of sexuality is—as man pumps, his power wanes. The dichotomy between active and passive, male and female, man and churn, disappears in a moment of lyric frenzy—"*Both* swayed and shook." The young man returns in line 7, not to power but to his place as object in a female fantasy. The narrative voice swings over: the man is a servant, sometimes useful, too often tired before the work's end. The lady's power is in the making: she bears the butter. The cost of love is dearer than our hero dreams.

RIDDLE 53

This riddle is a stumper. It seems to depend on linguistic or cultural knowledge lost to the modern world. Proposed solutions include *shield, scabbard, cross, harp, gallows, sword rack,* and *weapon chest.* The hall-borne creature, crafted of four woods, adorned with silver and gold, resembles a cross—the wolfshead-tree (an outlaw was a "wolfshead" and could be legally hunted and killed like a wolf—his "tree" was the gallows —thus Christ and his cross). Yet it receives weapons like the gold-hilted sword. It might be a scabbard or shield bearing the icon of the cross, but a composition of four woods would be neither stable nor strong. There was no Anglo-Saxon sword rack as far as we know. Swords were probably stowed and locked in a weapon chest: Does this one have the shape of the cross? Or do the four woods refer mystically to the cross (the four elements, the four corners of the world, the four gospels)? There is a patristic tradition for this sort of symbolism. But why would the cross receive swords? Short of transporting ourselves back to the Anglo-Saxon hall, we may never know.

RIDDLE 54

This creature is the *web and loom* of an Anglo-Saxon weaver. The loom has vertical warp-threads suspended by a horizontal beam. The threads are divided into alternate rows by a parting plank and kept taut by loom weights attached to their ends. This forms a natural shed through which the shuttle moves carrying the weft-thread. After the shuttle glides through the loom, the weft is struck tight by a toothed batten, the "small spears" of line 4 in the riddle. In the process of weaving, one of the alternate rows of weighted warp-threads dances up and down (pulled by a leash-rod) so that each pass of the shuttle moves on alternate sides of its strands. Thus the web in the riddle has a fixed and a furiously swinging foot. The bright tree may be either the loom with its colorful web or a distaff of flax or wool nearby. The loom's leaving, presumably a tapestry, is borne to the high hall of heroes. For more on the Anglo-Saxon loom, see Erika von Erhardt-Siebold, "The Old English Loom Riddles," listed in the Bibliography for Notes and Commentary. A famous classical description of weaving, perhaps known to the Old English riddler, occurs in book 6 of Ovid's *Metamorphoses* where Arachne, the most skilled of mortal weavers, and Pallas Athena pit their weaving skills against one another (6.52–64):

> The looms are set,
> The fine warp stretched, the web is bound to the beam,
> Reeds keep the threads apart, the shuttle threads
> Shrill through the woof, the busy fingers plying.
> With robes tucked up they speed the work, their hands,

Deft at the task, fly back and forth, the labor
Made less by eagerness. From the dark purple
The threads shade off to lighter pastel colors,
Like rainbow after storm, a thousand colors
Shining and blending, so the eye could never
Detect the boundary line, and yet the arcs
Are altogether different. Threads of gold
Were woven in, and each loom told a story.
[Trans. Rolfe Humphries]

RIDDLE 55

In the long list of solutions proposed for this riddle, birds predominate:
*swallows, gnats, starlings, raindrops, storm clouds, swifts, jackdaws, bees,
house martins, demons,* and *musical notes.* The dark-coated, song-bright
wind-riders who seem equally at home in the high wooded cliffs and the
halls of men are probably *swallows.* Swallows nest readily in the high
reaches of barns and open-eaved houses. They must have loved the commonly thatched roofs of medieval houses. Radbod, a ninth-century
Bishop of Utrecht, gives voice to the swallows' fondness for human habi-
tation in a Latin lyric which begins:

> I seek the winds that quicken,
>   Carry blooms, bud- and leaf-time,
> Build a brooding-bed in man's house
>   (Under eaves) where all eyes rest.
> Sweet fledglings I nuture till time ripens
>   And they bolt the nest, following
> My swift, tireless wings through summer.

The Anglo-Saxon Saint Guthlac is said to have been seen with swallows
sitting on his shoulders singing holy songs. The most famous Anglo-Saxon
hall-swallow appears in Bede's description of the seventh-century conver-

sion of King Edwin. Asked to compare the new Christian faith with the old Nordic faith, one of the king's counselors answers:

> Your Majesty, when we compare the present life of man on earth with that time of which we have no knowledge, it seems to me like the swift flight of a single sparrow through the banqueting-hall where you are sitting at dinner on a winter's day with your thanes and counsellors. In the midst there is a comforting fire to warm the hall; outside, the storms of winter rain or snow are raging. This sparrow flies swiftly in through one door of the hall, and out through another. While he is inside, he is safe from the winter storms; but after a few moments of comfort, he vanishes from sight into the wintry world from which he came. Even so, man appears on earth for a little while; but of what went before this life or of what follows, we know nothing. Therefore, if this new teaching has brought any more certain knowledge, it seems only right that we should follow it. [Trans. Leo Sherley-Price, rev. R. E. Latham, Bede's *A History of the English Church and People*, p. 127]

RIDDLE 56

The one-footed creature that works in a field and hauls water from a pit into the air is a *well sweep*, a device for drawing water from a well. The sweep is a long pole attached to an upright which serves as its fulcrum. The longer, lighter end of the sweep is connected to another pole or rope which lowers and raises the bucket in the well. The shorter end of the sweep may be weighted to help in raising the bucket. The riddle deals mostly in negatives. Like the speaker of Shakespeare's "Sonnet 130" ("My mistress' eyes are nothing like the sun"), the riddler takes delight here in saying what the creature is not—but like the sonneteer, he also has it both ways. Shakespeare's dark lady has eyes more bright for being unlike the sun. Mighty one-foot's ride may be short of the horse's, its haul light of the ship's—but it rides deep enough to draw water and quicken life. Like the dark lady, it is "rare / As any . . . belied with false compare."

This riddle celebrates the *chalice*—as riddle 46 perhaps does. Here the sacred "ring" ("anything round" in Old English) is passed to the communicants who celebrate the deep mystery of the Mass. The circle of gold "speaks" of Christ in two ways: it offers the sacred blood-wine of the Savior, and its body like Christ's is scored with wounds. The wounds are the icons and inscriptions, similar perhaps to those on the famous Tassilo chalice, an eighth-century gilt-bronze vessel of English or Anglo-Carolingian style. Like the cross in the Old English "Dream of the Rood," the chalice is both glorious token and wounded object. As it passes, "twisting, turning in the hands / Of proud men," its celebrants seem to reflect the torturers at the foot of the cross. Time collapses: Christ who was, is—and with the proper penetration of mystery, we become the celebrants-cum-crucifiers whom Christ has come to save. This is the larger riddle of God's grace.

RIDDLE 58

This riddle, set apart from the two main riddle groups in the Exeter Book, precedes a poem called "The Husband's Message," in which a personified rune staff (a piece of wood on which runes are incised) speaks to a woman, urging her to return by ship to her separated or exiled husband. "The Husband's Message" is itself enigmatic: the setting is dreamlike, the wood-singer's identity debated, the relationship between the protagonists unclear, and the runic message (consisting of five runes) open to a variety of interpretations. Some critics believe riddle 58 to be the opening portion of "The Husband's Message," and read the extended poem as a runic love letter sent by a man to his spouse or estranged lover; or as the message of a reed pen ripped from its home (like Christ) and brought to the greater glory of penning scripture and thus calling men to the higher kingdom; or as the statement of a wooden cross speaking to the church collective and individual, calling home the earthly "bride" of Christ. Less ambitious readers (myself included) solve the separate riddle as *rune staff* or *reed pen*, either of which may be taken from its watery home (the rune staff cut from willow or swamp cedar) and carved so that it bears a voiceless message privately to the reader in the mead-hall. If the creature is a reed pen, the riddle may derive in part from the fifth-century Latin "reed" riddle of Symphosius:

> I am the river-bank's darling and deep water's friend.
> Softly I sing to the Muses. Bathed in black,
> Guided by a scribe's hand, I am the tongue's messenger.

One pair of sea-hearty riddle solvers argues that the Old English creature is a piece of *kelp weed (laminaria digitata)* incised with runes; the runes are said to disappear when the kelp is dry and to reappear when it is wet again. The complete lack of medieval reference to such runic weed-wizardry however argues against the solution. Another farfetched guess, *a letter-beam cut from the stump of an old jetty*, seems less a solution than a stumped riddle solver's cry for quarter!

RIDDLE 59

Like the other bawdy riddles in the Exeter Book, this one has two solutions —one prim, one pornographic. The sexual identity of the tight treasure here is hardly hidden. Whether the proper solution is *helmet* or *shirt* remains in doubt. The mixture of colloquial, poetic, archaic, and just plain dirty diction creates a farcical tone in the riddle—as if a self-parodic sideshow for voyeurs were unfolding before the reader's eye. The mock decorum of the delicate "something" is undercut by the roisterous "shaggy" as the riddle ends with a chaotic circus of images (slick tricks, musclemen, dogs, jeweled queens). Inside the tent a Saxon show!

RIDDLE 60

The tunneling trickster of this riddle is probably a *borer* or *gimlet* which heats up as it spins in the hole and must be drawn out with a catch of cloth. Other suggestions include *flaming arrow, poker* or *fire-rod*, and *brand*. There is no question about the bawdy solution. The "southern thruster" is the subject of some debate. Is this a Welsh slave or a southern European hothead, a continental craftsman or the tool itself (there is a Viking "southern spear" thrown in "The Battle of Maldon")? Is "southern" also a bawdy directional reference? As the imagery of low-down travel dominates the riddle, the latter is a distinct possibility.

RIDDLE 61

The clear creature of this riddle fragment, cupped and kissed by carousing men, is a *glass beaker*. Continental and Anglo-Saxon glass cups, jars, and beakers are a common find in early English archaeological digs. The riddle has several motifs in common with the Latin "glass cup" riddle of the seventh-century English churchman Aldhelm:

> From cracked rocks I flowed as flames
> Shattered each dense heart of stone—
> The unleashed passion of furnace-heat.
> Now my shape is open and shines like ice.
> Men long to hold me, curl fingers round
> My slick form, clasp my neck—
> But I twist men's minds with wine-
> Sweet kisses on close lips and lure
> Stuttering footsteps to a fall.

Many of the Anglo-Saxon glass beakers are so shaped that they will not stand upright on the table. This may have been an invitation to the reckless drinking mentioned at the end of the riddle since the beakers once filled would have to be drained before they were put down.

RIDDLE 62

For a discussion of the two similarly structured, runic *ship* riddles in the Exeter Book, see the note to riddle 17. Both riddles are conceits built

A Feast of Creatures

upon the common Old English kenning of the ship as sea-horse. This smooth-prancing horse carries a bold warrior and a hawklike sail across the open sea-road. In riddle 62 the runes—represented by capital letters in the translation—initiate the spellings of hidden key-words which I take to be HOrse, MAn, HAwk, HEro, FAlcon, and sea TRack. "Man" and "hero" refer to the sailor, "hawk" and "falcon" to the sail (which with the oars is a "portion of power" and also the mast's or "lifter's joy"), and "sea track" to the wake of the ship. Because of the difficulty of the runes, earlier solutions for this riddle range from the ridiculous *(snake-eating bird and serpent* or *ring-tailed pheasant)* to the mundane *(man upon horseback with a hawk on his fist).* The *writing* solution offered for riddle 17 is also possible here. In the margin of the manuscript for this riddle, some waggish reader has scratched the runic equivalent of "Don't be cruel"—presumably because of the difficulty of the riddle.

RIDDLE 63

This is the second of two *onion* riddles—the other (riddle 23) a somewhat bawdier version of the slain slayer. This onion moves meekly from garden to carving bed where he suffers the indignity of slicing, shearing, and biting. A peace-lover at heart, he bites only his biters—but as the world seems to be populated with onion-eaters, he must be resolved to reducing the world to tears.

RIDDLE 64

This *creation* or *nature* riddle is a shortened and slightly more Puckish version of riddle 38. The spirit of nature which in-forms all things— middle-earth, moon, lakes, plains, angels, streams—seems here like Ariel "to fly, / To swim, to dive into the fire, to ride / On the curled clouds" (*The Tempest* 1.2.190). The flight at the end of the poem may mirror a metaphor of Christ's birdlike incarnation in the world in the Old English poem *Christ* (645 ff.):

So the great, loved bird risked flight,
Sometimes soaring to the homeland of angels,
Strong in spirit and might, sought his glory-home,
Sometimes swooped in a rush to earth, turning
Through holy grace to seek man's ground.

R I D D L E 65

This fragment is the second of two *book* or *Bible* riddles in the collection. Riddle 24 traces the detailed history of the book's life from ox-hide
to glittering scripture. Riddle 65, like the inscribed chalices of riddles 46
and 57, plays on the paradox of the mouthless speaker, here a treasured
teacher in the courts of men. Another possible "book" riddle, 91, elaborates upon the notion of the voiceless itinerant preacher.

R I D D L E 66

This bonelike wonder of the waves must be an *iceberg,* though previous
solutions have ranged as far afield as *petrified wood* and *Christ walking
upon the water!* The power and beauty of the wave-walker are underlined
by the starkness of the language and the bluntness of the concluding
paradox. The creature must have seemed a deadly splendor to the occasional Anglo-Saxon sailor who might have seen her in northern waters as
she drifted south from northeast Greenland toward Britain. For a different treatment of the iceberg, see riddle 31.

R I D D L E 67

Riddles 67 and 68 were once thought to be one riddle (the two together
solved with some editorial and mental gymnastics as *shepherd's pipe, rye
flute, harp, organistrum,* and *shuttle*), but a missing folio is now thought
to have separated the two. The round-necked chanteuse of this riddle
who "sings through her sides" is probably an Anglo-Saxon *lyre* similar to

the one discovered at Sutton Hoo. The Sutton Hoo lyre is a Germanic "round lyre" some thirty inches long, made of maple with pegs of poplar or willow. It has metal escutcheons on its shoulders like the "beautiful jewels" of the riddlic creature. The lyre was probably strung with gut; it has six strings and is thought to have been tuned to a pentatonic scale. This round lyre is called a "harp" in Old English poetry. The craft of the harper is described in "The Fortunes of Men":

> One sits with his harp at his lord's feet,
> Takes his treasure (a reward of rings),
> Plucks with his harp-nail, sweeps over strings,
> Shapes song: hall-thanes long for his melody.

Kings themselves sometimes played the lyre and sang in the mead-hall, as does the Danish king Hrothgar in *Beowulf* (2105 ff.):

> There was song-joy and story: the old Scylding,
> Wise in years and battle-fierce, sometimes spun
> Out of memory tales wound with the high pleasure
> Of harp-wood—songs of truth and sorrow,
> Marvellous spells woven by the great-hearted king,
> An old warrior lamenting his lost strength.

RIDDLE 68

This riddle fragment, once thought to be part of the preceding riddle, is now tentatively solved as *lighthouse*. A Latin "lighthouse" riddle by the seventh-century English churchman Aldhelm may give some clues about the shape of the original:

> On high cliffs where blue seas pound reefs
> And breakers swell on the ocean's plain,
> Man's craft has raised me, towering stone,
> To guide ships on safe sea-roads.
> I do not glide the sea-fields, drop oars,
> Or cut a curving furrow through the deep—

Yet, torchlight in tower, I lead wanderers
Whipped by savage waves, home to safe shores
When cloud-cover and cold fog wrap the stars' flame.

RIDDLE 69

The steep-cheeked weapon wrapped in gold and garnet is, like the creature
of riddle 18, a *sword*. The creature combines the stark beauty of an heirloom with the stinging strength of a slayer. The plain of bright flowers in
line 3 may be the field from which the ore is mined or the radiant iron
above the anvil (sparked by the smith's blows) from which the blade is
forged. The ring in line 9 is a sword-ring or ring-knob used on Anglo-
Saxon hilts to symbolize the warrior's liege-lord relationship.

RIDDLE 70

This is the last of three *ox* riddles which share certain motifs with the Latin
"ox" riddles of Aldhelm and Eusebius (see note to riddle 36). The stripling
ox is here drawn from the pleasure of its mother's four fountains (leaving
the herdsman to pull in its place for man's milk) and yoked to the hard life
of the plow. Drawing iron instead of milk, it moves without moaning—a
silent stoic. This same inexorable power is captured by Ted Hughes in his
description of "The Bull Moses" in *Lupercal:*

> And he took no pace but the farmer
> Led him to take it, as if he knew nothing
> Of the ages and continents of his fathers
>
> . . . .
>
> The weight of the sun and the moon and the world hammered
> To a ring of brass through his nostrils.
> He would raise
> His streaming muzzle and look out over the meadows,
> But the grasses whispered nothing awake, the fetch
> Of the distance drew nothing to momentum

In the locked black of his powers. He came strolling gently back,
Paused neither toward the pig-pens on his right,
Nor toward the cow-byres on his left: something
Deliberate in his leisure, some beheld future
Founding in his quiet.

RIDDLE 71

The creature which is hauled from its homeland, stripped and reshaped,
forced to battle against its will for a grim lord is a *spear* or *lance*. Like its
brother the ram in riddle 51, it is ripped from innocence and made to
ravage in man's murderous world. The riddle is a strange combination of
heroic celebration and grotesque irony. Bright glory is a bit dimmed when
warriors become marauders; and weapons, muggish tools for bashing brains.
The unnamed "one" that "breaks ready for the road home" at the end of
the poem is the soul of an expiring recipient of the spear and spear-man's
quest for glory. Many of the themes of the riddle—the protagonist's separation from his land and family, its fall from innocence, its reluctant role as
slayer—may be found in the Old English "Dream of the Rood" where the
wood made to bear Christ similarly recalls its wrenching fate:

> It was long ago—I remember I was ripped
> From the forest's edge, torn from my trunk,
> Seized by fierce enemies, sheared and shaped,
> Forced to raise hard criminals high—a dumb show.

The rood wins salvation through suffering, but the riddlic spear has only
a marauder's joy and a lunger's glory.

RIDDLE 72

This riddle has given the riddle solvers fits. Among the proposed solutions
are *cuttlefish, swan, quill pen, water, siren, soul, sea-eagle,* and *ship's figurehead.* The quill for example might dip in and out of the sea of ink and fly

through the air to the shore of the page; the water might soar as clouds, fly as rain, make war as ice, dive as a sea-stream, and run on the shore as a river. The figurehead in the form of a girl would charge the waves like a great warrior, swoop through the air and dive through the spray, stand up on the shore as part of a beached boat or a detached prow (figureheads were sometimes detached in order not to offend guardian shore spirits). But perhaps the real answer has yet to be found!

RIDDLE 73

The letters in the second line (which are runes in the original) read backwards give the solution to the riddle—PISS! For a long time the riddle was thought to be two separate riddles or (according to different readings of the runes) some strange creature—*a wandering hound dog, Mrs. Elk separated from her husband, a lonely hen,* or *Christ as a hunter in pursuit of sin.* But the irreverent solution is now the generally accepted one. The riddle turns on the visual distinction between men's and women's modes of urination, a motif found occasionally in the folklore of certain primitive traditions.

RIDDLE 74

This footless, fixed creature of the sea with its bone-skin and sweet flesh is an *oyster.* The sea-mouth is caught, cracked, and hauled to its own door of doom (man's mouth!). The "eater eaten" motif echos that of the "biter bitten" in riddle 63. My own recent oyster riddle provides an interesting modern analogue:

> My house is salt,
> My salt is stone;
> I hold my hostel
> Of mantle-spun bone.
> I welcome sailors
> On the drifted wind—
> Floaters, feasts,

A Feast of Creatures
208

Ushered in
To soft tables.
I am able
To spin orbs
Like ice-milk
For a woman's ear.
I fear man,
The snail,
The tentacled star.
I am the sea's
Tiresian queen—
Still without sight.
I am the cripple
That cradles light.

[*College English* 35 (1974): 469]

RIDDLE 75

Clues in this riddle fragment suggest that the creature is a migratory fish with a strange, cunning power used to kill other creatures below the waves. This might be the *lamprey,* a common Anglo-Saxon catch, which migrates from the sea to fresh water to spawn and returns to the sea again—and which kills its underwater prey by leeching onto it with a funnel-shaped mouth while rasping off the victim's flesh with its lingual teeth. Hauled from the deep, it must have seemed a savage catch.

RIDDLE 76

Although this creature sounds like a cross between a musical battle-sword and a flowerpot, it is actually a *horn.* In the battle-rush it sings out with a clarion call. At the supper table it bears wood-blooms and the bee's delight —mead made from honey. It can both sing and reward singers (Anglo-Saxon scops) with the gift of brew. Tongue in cheek, it laments because the hands of the noble lady who serves its mead are a little too honeyed! Riddle 12 is a companion "horn" riddle.

This suffering servant, bound to its perch, buffeted by winds, is a *weathercock*. Because Peter denied Christ three times before cockcrow (Luke 22:60), in the Middle Ages iron cocks were placed on church towers (and even on crossroad crucifixes) as a sign of Christ's coming and as a call to vigilance and repentance. So Ambrose says in his "Hymn at Cockcrow" ("Aeterne Rerum Conditor"):

> When the cock crows, hope comes,
> Health graces the heart-sick,
> The sword of plunder is put down,
> And faith returns to the fallen.

The watchful cock of the church tower apparently gave rise to the medieval weathercock. The riddlic description of the wind-swung bird is one of the earliest. The riddler has artfully created a Christlike cock perched on its nail, twisting in torment, bound to its fate, serving faithfully, a gift to men. Buffeted by storm, it marks the wind, and in that act of charting rises above its fate. Its act of passion, like Christ's, is both literally and spiritually transcendent as it swings high above men.

RIDDLE 78

The few remaining clues of this fragment suggest that the strange, ground-gobbling creature may be a *harrow*. The Anglo-Saxon harrow pictured in the Bayeux Tapestry was a sharp-toothed implement dragged across fields after the initial plowing to break up clods of soil.

RIDDLE 79

This riddle deals with the origin and outcome of some rare metal used in the making of artifacts and coins—probably *gold*. It may have its roots in a fifth-century Latin "money" riddle by Symphosius:

Earth-child I was, skulking in ground
Till smelt-flames offered a new name and price:
No longer earth, I can purchase the earth.

The gold ore in the Old English riddle is ripped from its homeland,
wrought by a legendary smith (probably Tubal-Cain), smelted and shaped
to bear man's icons and inscriptions. Its wounds are many, yet paradoxically
for this grim passage its power is great. Unable to defy miner, smelter,
artisan—it reaps revenge on the collective shaper, man. Separated from its
family, it separates and enthralls the family of man. So the *Beowulf* poet
says that "the power of treasure, gold in the ground / Will take us, hide
it or heed it as we may" (2764 ff.). The riddlic power of gold to destroy
its human shaper is oft lamented in later English poetry, most forcefully
perhaps in George Herbert's seventeenth-century sonnet "Avarice":

> Money, thou bane of bliss, and source of woe,
>> Whence comest thou, that thou art so fresh and fine?
>> I know thy parentage is base and low:
> Man found thee poor and dirty in a mine.
> Surely thou didst so little contribute
>> To this great kingdom, which thou now has got,
>> That he was fain, when thou wert destitute,
> To dig thee out of thy dark cave and grot:
> Then forcing thee by fire he made thee bright:
>> Nay, thou hast got the face of man; for we
>> Have with our stamp and seal transferred our right:
> Thou art the man, and man but dross to thee.
>> Man calleth thee his wealth, who made thee rich;
>> And while he digs out thee, falls in the ditch.

RIDDLE 80

This mother of all earth-creatures, weaver of world-children's might, is
water. Pliny, in book 31 of his *Natural History,* describes water as the
greatest of creatures (31.1):

Nature the Creator gives her tireless strength to waves, billows, tides, and swift river-currents. The truth is that nothing is stronger than water—it is lord of all things. It swallows land, destroys fire, climbs into the sky where it rules, choking the life-quickening spirit with its blanket of clouds, shaking out thunder-bolts and waging its own civil war in the world. What can be stranger than water standing in the sky? Not only can it rise, it can suck up schools of fish, even stones, lifting a weight not its own. Water also falls back to earth to become the source and spring of all things. This is Nature's miracle—for crops to grow, for trees and shrubs to thrive, water soars to the sky and brings down to plants the breath of life —so that even all earth-powers are part of water's sustaining might. What mortal could name the countless examples of water's powers?

In the Old English riddle, water is the great mother of all creation, allied (however primitive her nature) with a brooding Trinity. From the womb of water issue the myriad shapes of creation. Water bears and sustains, soothes and punishes. Herself a shape-shifter—ice, snow, rain, hail, stream, lake, sea—she dies and is born again, both mother and child (for a similar theme see the end of "iceberg" riddle 31). Two medieval Latin riddles by the seventh-century English churchman Aldhelm deal with the same subject:

Water

Who would not wonder at my strange lot?
Strong enough to carry a thousand oaks,
Yet a wagon pierced by the smallest needle.
Sky-birds and sea-fish owe their origin to me.
Nature has ceded me a third of the earth.

*   *   *

A Spring

I creep through earth-caves, winding my swift,
Silent way—curling, circling through rock-veins.
My skill (without sense, without life) is this:

I shape creation. Who can count the myriad
Creatures I quicken? Their number is greater
Than the stars flashing, twirling through heaven
Or the sands hauled by the wave-washed sea.

RIDDLE 81

This *fish and river* riddle is based on the fifth-century Latin riddle of
Symphosius:

> This house echoes with a loud, clear sound
> On earth, resounds while its guest is silent.
> Bound together, guest and home course and run.

The Old English riddle draws upon the Latin motif of the loud house with
its quiet creature, then elaborates on a theme of common and contrastive
movement. It concludes with a vital paradox: hauled from its house, the
creature dies.

RIDDLE 82

The motif here is based on a fifth-century Latin riddle by Symphosius:

> Step up and see what you won't believe:
> A one-eyed man with a thousand heads.
> He sells what he has. Can he buy what he lacks?

The solution, fortunately provided in the Latin title, is *one-eyed seller of
garlic*. This sort of deliberately obscure and confounding riddle is what
Archer Taylor calls a neck-riddle:

> Another very curious variety of enigma consists in a description of
> a scene that can be interpreted only by the one who sets the puzzle.
> The terms used are not confusing, but the situation itself seems

inexplicable. In many northern European versions of such puzzles the speaker saves his neck by the riddle, for the judge or executioner has promised release in exchange for a riddle that cannot be guessed. ["The Varieties of Riddles," in *Philologica: The Malone Anniversary Studies*, ed. Thomas A. Kirby and Henry Bosley Woolf, p. 6]

While not all neck riddles are designed to escape the hangman, certainly all are designed to confuse the solver. Without the gift of Symphosius's title, we should never have solved this one.

RIDDLE 83

This is a plain *bellows* riddle—its bawdier cousin is at riddle 35. The creature is seized by a strong servant, muscled and pumped so the cold wind, the "tooth of heaven," sings through its eye. Like a hysterical prima donna, the creature continues to puff up and pass out, reviving on air to repeat its monstrously ocular song.

RIDDLE 84

This is the first of two *inkhorn* riddles in the collection—the other is riddle 89. Both riddles trace the horn's history from its natural home on the stag's head through its capture and cutting by a craftsman to its place of suffering on the scribe's desk. Although both riddles are a lament for things past, this riddle seems more properly elegiac with its shifting time-frames, its brooding sense of memory, its contrast between past glory and present suffering, and its focus upon the separation of brothers (the two horns) and the resulting sense of isolation and loss. Riddle 89 on the other hand has heroic elements such as its straightforward narrative sequence, its celebration of the lord-stag's powers and the liege-horn's service and stoic acceptance of fate, and its kenning reference to the beasts of battle. Both riddles attempt to spin out the horn's life in a sympathetic song quite different from the only other early "inkhorn" riddle, a Latin offering by the eighth-century English Abbot Eusebius of Wearmouth:

> Once a fateful weapon, I rode with the arms
> Of the bull, a bold-riding battle-crest.
> Now my carved belly holds a bitter drink
> Though my belch seems bright, sweet, clean.

A medieval recipe for the making of ink is included in the note to riddle 89.

RIDDLE 85

If the ending of this riddle fragment means that the leather creature is used at the dinner table, it may be a *leather bottle* or *flask* like the one fashioned by the shoemaker and leather-worker in Aelfric's *Colloquy*—but the clues here are so scant, it is difficult to sustain any solution.

RIDDLE 86

This is the only Latin riddle in the Exeter Book. The reasons for its inclusion in the collection remain uncertain. Tentative solutions have seemed as surreal as the riddle itself. One solver argues that the various meanings of Latin *lupus* ("wolf," "pike," "hops") are the subject of the riddle. Another sees in the combination of Old English "ewu" and "wulf" ("ewe" and "wolf") a reference to the final letters in the name *Cynewulf*, a possible but unlikely riddle poet. Another word-player suggests that "wulf" and "flys" together ("wulflys," "fleece of wool") may refer to the *woolen web on an Anglo-Saxon vertical loom*. The three wolves would then represent the odd and even sides of the warp tormenting the weft; the four feet would combine the two of the loom with the two of the warp (also called "feet" in riddle 54); the seven eyes might be pairs of ring-shaped, clay loom weights. Another solver sees in the riddle the *Lamb of God* who destroys the wolflike Devil, who stands with the Trinity on Calvary (or as seems more likely, with the wolfish thieves), whose feet are the four Gospels, and whose eyes are the seven eyes of the apocalyptic Lamp or the seven Spirits of God sent forth in Revelation. Part of the difficulty may be due to the complexity of cultural meanings attached to the wolf. Originally the wolf was a sacred animal associated with Woden, but with the advent of Christianity the wolf became a diabolical figure. The wolf as battle-warrior in the comitatal pack was respected and revered, but the savage lone wolf was feared and hated. Early admiration for the wolf seems reflected in its use in names like Beowulf and Cynewulf, but the word "wulf" comes eventually to mean "criminal" or "outcast" in Old English. This in turn is complicated by the redemptive idea of Christ as wolf, reflected for example in riddle 53, where the cross is called a "wolfshead-tree." How any or all of this may enter into the riddle and into possibly related poems like "Wulf and Eadwacer" is still a matter of some conjecture. Meanwhile the riddlic wolf and lamb continue to perplex even the most ambitious of solvers.

RIDDLE 87

This is the second of two *key* riddles in the Exeter collection; a somewhat lustier version occurs at riddle 42. This key begins its history with hammer and forge, then leaps to its tongue-in-cheek confrontation with a slightly sensuous, brass foe. The conjunction of lock and key recalls the sexual entendre of riddle 42. Does "the gift of slaughter, the joy of gold" refer to a battlefield treasure hauled to the hoard, or to the bedroom gifts of a gold-adorned woman waiting for her conqueror's sexual "slaughter" (like the implicit other "sword-slaughter" of riddle 18)? Or does the mixture imply a riddlic world in which gold is as sensual as delight is rich?

RIDDLE 88

This riddle fragment can be solved only in Old English—its answer is *boc*, which means either "beech" or "book." The "boast of brown snufflers" is beech mast, fodder for pigs. Lines 1b–3a celebrate the tree in the wood. Line 3b refers to a secret love letter on a strip of bark or perhaps to some literary romance. The treasure of line 4 is a gold-adorned book. The weapon of line 5 is probably a beech-shield adorned with a ring that signifies the bearer's liege-lord bond.

RIDDLE 89

This is the second of two *inkhorn* riddles—the other is riddle 84. While the earlier riddle is highly elegiac, this riddle has its heroic elements. The horn speaks first not of its present suffering but of the former glory of its lord. While it uses this history to explain its lot, it does not seem haunted by the past. Its suffering is physical; it endures the pains of cutting, scraping, shaping, swallowing wood and stained water (ink), and the darting birdlike quill with stoic equanimity. The battle-companion of the wolf in line 20 is the eagle or raven (these three are the carrion-eaters or "beasts of battle" in Old English poetry) whose quill now plunders ink from the horn's belly. A similar description of quill and ink occurs in "Bible" or "book" riddle 24:

> Now the bird's once wind-stiff joy
> Darts often to the horn's dark rim,
> Sucks wood-stain, steps back again.

A medieval recipe for the making of ink is contained in the twelfth-century *Diverse Arts* (2.38) of Theophilus, a German Benedictine:

> To make ink, cut for yourself some wood of the hawthorn—in April or May before they produce blossom or leaves—collect them together in small bundles and allow them to lie in the shade for two, three or four weeks until they are fairly well dried out.
> Then have some wooden mallets, and with them pound these thorns on a hard piece of wood until you can completely peel off the bark, which you immediately put in a barrel full of water. When you have filled two, three, four or five barrels with bark and

water, allow them to stand like this for eight days until the water has drawn off all the sap of the bark. Then put this water into a very clean pot or into a cauldron, place it on the fire and heat it. From time to time, put some of this bark into the pot so that, if there is any sap left in it, it can be boiled out, and, when you have heated it for a little, take it out and put in some more. This done, boil down what remains of the water to a third [of its original quantity], pour it from this pot into a smaller one and continue to heat it until it becomes black and begins to thicken, taking particular care that you do not add any water except that which was mixed with the sap. When you see it become thick, add a third part of pure wine, put it in two or three new pots and continue to heat it until you see that it develops a kind of skin at the top.

Then lift these pots off the fire and put them in the sun until the black ink resolves itself from the red dregs. Afterwards, take some small, carefully sewn, parchment bags like bladders, pour the pure ink into them and hang them up in the sun until it is completely dried. When it is dried, take from it as much as you want, mix it with wine over a fire, add a little iron vitriol and write. If, as a result of carelessness, the ink is not black enough, take a piece of iron, an inch thick, put it on the fire until it is red hot and then throw it into the ink. [Trans. C. R. Dodwell, Theophilus' *De Diversis Artibus/ The Various Arts*, pp. 34–35]

Hardy modern scribes and eclectic cooks might like to try the recipe.

RIDDLE 90

The few surviving phrases of this riddle fragment show a resemblance to the comparatives of *nature* or *creation* riddles 38 and 64.

RIDDLE 91

This much-debated riddle is a fit conclusion to the Exeter collection. Its creature claims to be well known and often in the keeping of men, but it has yet to be identified to the satisfaction of all. A number of questions continue to plague the would-be solvers. What is the nature of the creature's journey? Why does it rest with the high and low? How does it come to a quiet keeping? What is the plunderer's joy that it bears? Who or what is the plunderer? How does the creature proclaim wisdom without voice? Why are its tracks sometimes hard to follow? Solutions range from *soul* to *wandering singer* and include *moon, quill pen, book, prostitute*—even *riddle* itself. *Dream* is another possibility. Is the plunderer's joy the book's gold, the pen's ink, the moon's treasure of light, the singer's studded lyre, the prostitute's favors, the riddler's mystery, the spirit's quickness, or the splendors of dream? These questions continue to haunt the solvers. The creature seems so near—yet still strangely undiscovered. Guess what it is!

BIBLIOGRAPHY FOR
NOTES AND COMMENTARY

Readers should refer to the note at the head of the Notes and Commentary section and bear in mind: (1) that translations from classical and medieval sources that occur in the Notes and Commentary are my own unless otherwise indicated; and (2) that quotations from postmedieval, premodern sources are often normalized to show modern spellings (and occasionally alternate punctuations) when they appear in the Notes and Commentary.

Aelfric. *Aelfric's Colloquy.* 2d ed. Edited by G. N. Garmonsway. London: Methuen and Co. 1947.

Alcuin. "He Laments His Lost Nightingale" ["De Luscinia"]. In *The Oxford Book of Medieval Latin Verse,* edited by F. J. E. Raby, p. 106. Oxford: Clarendon Press, 1959.

Aldhelm. *Aldhelmi Opera.* Edited by R. Ehwald. *Monumenta Germaniae Historica, Auctores Antiquissimi,* vol. 15. Berlin: Weidmann, 1919. (On the question of Aldhelm's authorship of the storm poem "Lector, casses catholice," see also M. Lapide and M. Herron, *Aldhelm: The Prose Works* [Cambridge: D. S. Brewer, 1979], pp. 16–18.) *See also* Glorie, editor.

Ambrose. "Hymn at Cockcrow" ["Aeterne Rerum Conditor"]. In *The Oxford Book of Medieval Latin Verse,* edited by F. J. E. Raby, pp. 8–9. Oxford: Clarendon Press, 1959.

Bede. *A History of the English Church and People [Historia Ecclesiastica Gentis Anglorum].* Translated by Leo Sherley-Price, revised by R. E. Latham. Baltimore, Md.: Penguin, 1968.

Blake, William. *The Poetry and Prose of William Blake.* Edited by David V. Erdman. Commentary by Harold Bloom. New York: Doubleday and Co., 1965.

Caesar. *The Gallic War [De Bello Gallico].* Edited by H. J. Edwards. Loeb Library Series. Cambridge and London: Harvard University Press and Heinemann, 1917.

Donne, John. *The Poems of John Donne.* Edited by Herbert J. C. Grierson. 2 vols. Oxford: Clarendon Press, 1912.

Dryden, John, translator. Vergil's *Aeneid.* In *The Works of John Dryden,* vol. 3. Edited by James Kinsley. Oxford: Clarendon Press, 1958.

Erhardt-Siebold, Erika von. "The Old English Loom Riddles." In *Philologica: The Malone Anniversary Studies,* edited by Thomas A. Kirby and Henry Bosley Woolf, pp. 9–17. Baltimore, Md.: Johns Hopkins University Press, 1949.

Eusebius. *See* Glorie, editor.

Giraldus Cambrensis. *Topography of Ireland [Topographia Hibernica].* In *Giraldi Cambrensis Opera,* edited by James F. Dimock, Rolls Series 21, part 5, pp. 3–204. London, 1867.

Glorie, Fr., editor. *Variae Collectiones Aenigmatum Merovingicae Aetatis.* In *Corpus Christianorum, Series Latina,* vols. 133, 133A (includes the Latin riddle collections of Symphosius, Aldhelm, Tatwine, and Eusebius). Turnhout: Brepols, 1968.

Herbert, George. *The Works of George Herbert.* Edited by F. E. Hutchinson. Oxford: Clarendon Press, 1941.

Hopkins, Gerard Manley. *The Poems of Gerard Manley Hopkins.* 4th ed. Edited by W. H. Gardner and N. H. MacKenzie. New York: Oxford University Press, 1967.

Hughes, Ted. *The Hawk in the Rain.* New York: Harper and Brothers, 1957.
———. *Lupercal.* New York: Harper and Brothers, 1960.

Keats, John. *The Poetical Works of John Keats.* 2d. ed. Edited by H. W. Garrod. Oxford: Clarendon Press, 1956.

Klaeber, Fr., editor. *Beowulf and The Fight at Finnsburg.* 3d ed. with supplements. Boston: D. C. Heath, 1950.

Krapp, George Philip, and Dobbie, Elliott Van Kirk, editors. *The Anglo-Saxon Poetic Records.* 6 vols. New York: Columbia University Press, 1931–53.

Melville, Herman. *Collected Poems of Herman Melville.* Edited by Howard P. Vincent. Chicago: Packard and Co., 1947.

Ovid. *Metamorphoses.* Translated by Rolfe Humphries. Bloomington, Ind.: Indiana University Press, 1955.

Pliny. *Natural History [Historia Naturalis].* Edited by H. Rackham and W. S. Jones.

10 vols. Loeb Library Series. Cambridge and London: Harvard University Press and Heinemann, 1938–62.

Radbod. "The Swallow" ["De Hirundine"]. In *Mediaeval Latin Lyrics*, edited by Helen Waddell, p. 132. London: Constable, 1948.

Rich, Adrienne. *Leaflets: Poems 1965–68*. New York: W. W. Norton and Co., 1969.

Rowland, Beryl. *Birds with Human Souls*. Knoxville, Tenn.: University of Tennessee Press, 1978.

Shakespeare, William. *The Complete Works*. General editor, Alfred Harbage. Baltimore, Md.: Penguin, 1969.

Shelley, Percy Bysshe. *Poetical Works*. Edited by Thomas Hutchinson. New York: Oxford University Press, 1969.

Stevens, Wallace. *The Collected Poems of Wallace Stevens*. New York: Alfred A. Knopf, 1965.

Symphosius. *See* Glorie, editor.

Tatwine. *See* Glorie, editor.

Taylor, Archer. "The Varieties of Riddles." In *Philologica: The Malone Anniversary Studies*, edited by Thomas A. Kirby and Henry Bosley Woolf, pp. 1–8. Baltimore, Md.: Johns Hopkins University Press, 1949.

Theophilus. *The Various Arts [De Diversis Artibus]*. Translated by C. R. Dodwell. London: Thomas Nelson, 1961.

Whitman, Walt. *Leaves of Grass*. Edited by Sculley Bradley and Harold W. Blodgett. New York: W. W. Norton and Co., 1973.

Williams, William Carlos. *Paterson*. New York: New Directions, 1963.

Williamson, Craig, editor. *The Old English Riddles of the Exeter Book*. Chapel Hill, N.C.: University of North Carolina Press, 1977.

——. "Two Riddles." *College English* 35 (1974): 468–69.

Yeats, William Butler. *The Collected Poems of W. B. Yeats*. London: Macmillan and Co., 1965.

INDEX OF SOLUTIONS

Indexed below are commonly favored solutions along with a selection of other proposed solutions that still find some support among modern editors and riddle solvers.

Riddle	Favored Solution	Other Proposed Solutions
1	Wind	Storm
2	Uncertain	Bell, Millstone, Flail, Quill Pen
3	Shield	
4	Sun	
5	Whistling Swan	
6	Nightingale	Chough, Jay, Jackdaw, Thrush, Wood Pigeon
7	Cuckoo	
8	Barnacle Goose	
9	Cup of Wine or Spirits	Gold, Night
10	Ox	
11	Ten Chickens	Ten Fingers
12	Horn	
13	Fox	Badger, Hedgehog, Porcupine, Weasel
14	Anchor	
15	Uncertain	Weapon Chest, Ballista, Fortress, Forge, Inkwell
16	Amphora	
17	Ship	Falconry, Writing

Riddle	Favored Solution	Other Proposed Solutions
18	Sword	Sword-Swallow (Hawk), Phallus
19	Plow	
20	Charles's Wain and the Circling Stars	Month of December
21	Bow	
22	Magpie	Jay
23	Onion	
24	Bible, Book	
25	Mead	
26	Uncertain	Horn of Yew, Wine Cask, Lyre, Damascened Sword, John Barleycorn
27	Moon and Sun	
28	Tree, Wood	
29	Bagpipe	
30	Ship	
31	Iceberg	
32	Rake	
33	Coat of Mail	
34	Ship	
35	Bellows	
36	Ox (Bull Calf)	
37	Uncertain	Speech, Dream, Death, Time, Moon, Cloud, Day
38	Creation, Nature	
39	Water	Earth, Nature
40	Cock and Hen	
41	Soul and Body	
42	Key	Dagger Sheath
43	Bread Dough	
44	Lot and His Family	
45	Bookworm	
46	Chalice	Paten
47	Oven	Bookcase, Falcon Cage, Pen
48	Fire	
49	Quill Pen and Fingers	
50	Flail	Broom, Well Buckets, Yoke of Oxen

Riddle	Favored Solution	Other Proposed Solutions
51	Battering Ram	Spear, Cross
52	Churn	
53	Uncertain	Weapon Chest, Sword Rack, Cross, Scabbard, Shield
54	Web and Loom	
55	Swallows	Starlings, Swifts, Jackdaws, House Martins, Gnats, Bees, Raindrops, Musical Notes
56	Well Sweep	
57	Chalice	
58	Uncertain	Rune Staff, Reed Pen, Cross, Kelp Weed
59	Helmet	Shirt
60	Borer, Gimlet	Brand, Poker, Fire-Rod, Flaming Arrow
61	Glass Beaker	
62	Ship	Falconry, Writing
63	Onion	
64	Creation, Nature	
65	Bible, Book	
66	Iceberg	
67	Lyre	Shepherd's Pipe, Shuttle (in conjunction with following riddle)
68	Lighthouse	
69	Sword	
70	Ox	
71	Spear, Lance	
72	Uncertain	Ship's Figurehead, Water, Cuttlefish, Siren, Soul, Swan, Sea-Eagle, Quill Pen
73	Piss	Hound, Elk, Christ (each with a different reading of the runes)
74	Oyster	
75	Lamprey	
76	Horn	
77	Weathercock	
78	Harrow	
79	Gold	Ore, Money
80	Water	
81	Fish and River	

Riddle	Favored Solution	Other Proposed Solutions
82	One-Eyed Seller of Garlic	
83	Bellows	
84	Inkhorn	
85	Uncertain	Leather Bottle, Flask
86	Uncertain	Woolen Web and Loom, Lamb of God, Cynewulf
87	Key	Keyhole
88	Beech / Book	
89	Inkhorn	
90	Nature, Creation	
91	Uncertain	Book, Wandering Singer, Moon, Quill Pen, Dream, Riddle, Prostitute, Soul

ALPHABETICAL
INDEX OF SOLUTIONS

Solutions from the previous index are listed here alphabetically. Favored solutions are listed in roman type; other proposed solutions in italics.

Index of Solutions

229

A Note on the Translator

Craig Williamson grew up in Indiana and studied at Stanford, Harvard, and the University of Pennsylvania. His fields of expertise are medieval English literature and linguistic anthropology. He is editor of *The Old English Riddles of the Exeter Book,* a language text on which the present translations are based, translator of Léopold Sédar Senghor's *Selected Poems / Poésies Choisies,* and author of a book of poems, *African Wings.* He spent several years working in Africa for the American Friends' Service Committee. Currently he is Associate Professor of English Literature at Swarthmore College where he teaches medieval and modern poetry.